Dedica

This book is a heartfelt dedication to the incredible individuals who have had an enormous impact on my life. First and foremost, I dedicate this story to my strong and beautiful mother, Gloria. Her unwavering love, support, and encouragement (along with that of my father, Bill) have shaped me into the strong, independent, and adventurous woman that I am today.

I also dedicate this book to my amazing and courageous brother, *Mark Christopher S* (born *Michael William Bayliss*). Although we never had the opportunity to meet in person, your resilience and determination have inspired me in so many ways. I am blessed to be your little sister.

Additionally, I would like to extend my deepest gratitude to *Mark Blundell* and *Clint Nix*. Your love, friendship, and generosity of sharing played a pivotal role in spiritually bringing Gloria's son into her life, and mine. Without your support, we would have never had the opportunity to know and cherish this special connection.

To Gloria's cousin, *Pauline*. Thank you for sharing your memories of an amazing voyage with me, your stories added a new dimension to my understanding of my mother's journey, and she always thought the world of you.

To my extraordinary children, *Georgia* and *Cameron*.

Each of you at a very tender age has played a unique role in shaping this story. I cherish each and every moment we have shared throughout this journey. I could not have done it without you, you truly are the wind beneath my wings.

And finally, to my darling husband *Simon*:

Thank you for being the anchor in my life and giving me my happily ever after.

Introduction

O ctober 5th 2022, a surge of exhilaration courses through my veins. Glancing down at my boarding pass I catch sight of the golden words "boarding time 1.30pm." Merely thirty fleeting minutes now separate me from embarking on this journey. It marks not only the beginning but also the culmination of a profound and extraordinary voyage which in fact began some fifty-eight years earlier, before I was even born. Yet here I stand on the dockside of San Diego Bay, about to board Holland America Line's cruise ship Noordam; but this is not just a cruise, this is the final chapter of an immense circle of love and a cherished cargo being carried on its way to its final destination.

By my side stands a bubbling bundle of excitement, my son Cameron, aged ten. He is my constant companion in both my travels and educational journey. Together we have embraced a unique approach to learning, one that we affectionately refer to as world-schooling, one which expands Cameron's knowledge beyond the classroom and allows us to explore the world while immersing ourselves in different countries and cultures. This chapter of our own story commenced just a few days earlier when we flew from London to San Diego, giving ourselves the opportunity of basking in the warm Californian sunshine for five blissful days and allowing ourselves to acclimatise to the eight-hour time difference before embarking on the upcoming voyage.

In our personal narrative, we find ourselves finally about to rejoin a transpacific cruise which initially set sail in March 2020, two and a half years earlier. However, the unforeseen outbreak of the Covid pandemic forced numerous Pacific ports on our itinerary to shut their borders to us, leaving us along with another 800 passengers marooned aboard the MS Maasdam in the vast Pacific Ocean for four weeks. That tale, though captivating in its own right, is not to detract from this one, however suffice to say that after a two-and-a-half-year wait we are brimming with anticipation and eagerness to set foot on the Noordam to embark on this long-awaited adventure together.

Our hearts have yearned to explore the enchanting islands we were forced to sail past in 2020, and the allure of paradise, turquoise seas and powder white sands beckons us, filling us with huge excitement. With each passing moment our anticipation intensifies, for we know that this journey will be etched into our memories forever and will be further testament to the unyielding spirit of adventure which now transcends three generations of our family.

The past two and a half years have brought about profound changes in my life, those of both love and loss. The devastating 2020 pandemic robbed me of both my parents within a span of seven months. Now as I stand on the precipice of boarding this ship with Cameron, I feel overwhelmed with emotion (although I hide it well for his sake), for on this voyage I carry a very precious cargo, the cremated remains of my beloved mother Gloria.

As the seconds tick on to 1.30pm our boarding group is called forward for check-in, and I silently whisper, "come on, Mum, it's time to go home." It is then with a mix of excitement and reverence that I step aboard the Noordam, our floating home for the next five weeks. Our final destination; Sydney, Australia. The voyage ahead is shrouded in an element of mystery, yet I feel hopeful for whatever lies beyond the horizon, a journey which will intertwine adventure with remembrance. I 'may' even get time to write a book, a true story which will be a testament to the resilience of human spirit and the enduring power of love. I carry with me little in the way of personal possessions, but rather an unwavering determination to honour a legacy, to speak an unspoken truth, and to create my own special ending to the story, a conclusion brimming with happiness and fulfilment.

Gloria was my mum, a dedicated and popular State Registered Nurse hailing from Worthing on the south coast of England. In the spring of 1964, at the tender age of twenty-five, she embarked on a life-altering voyage from the waters of Southampton as a Ten Pound Pom, seeking a fresh start in the sun-kissed lands of Australia. Little did anyone know the extraordinary twist of fate that awaited her; a narrative woven with adventure, romance, and heartache, connecting lives across the globe through the unbreakable bonds of love – none more so than the bond of love between a mother and child, along with the untangling of a huge web of lies created by the Catholic Church.

For years, I have carried the intention of penning my mother's remarkable story, however, the constraints of time have always hindered my progress. Yet, as I embarked on this new journey along-side my young son and carrying my late mother's ashes, a newfound determination surged within me. I felt compelled to finally put pen to paper and share not just her, but ultimately 'our' story.

The time had come to honour my mum's legacy, to immortalise her adventures and the profound impact they had on countless lives. Through the written word, I aimed to capture the essence of her spirit, the resilience that carried her through life's trials, and the love that radiated from her being, and ultimately to her children.

As Cameron and I sailed away from San Diego's shores that first night, I felt compelled to share our story, to inspire others, and to ensure that Gloria's legacy lived on in the hearts of those who read these words.

Before we focus on an ending though, we have to start at the beginning, and this is where this story starts for me ...

CHAPTER 1

First Glimpses of Australia

My childhood was a happy but simple one; we didn't have much and yet we wanted for nothing. I was the younger of two daughters born just twenty-one months apart, and we grew up in a small terrace house in Lancing, a village on the south coast of England. Our parents, Gloria and Bill, had by 1960s and '70s standards, married and had children quite late in life. They met in 1967, married in 1968, had my sister Marie in 1969, and I came along in November 1970. It was a busy four years for them. Mum was thirty-two when I was born and in those days throughout her pregnancy she was referred to as a 'geriatric' mother. Certainly, I remember at school my mum was the oldest out of all my friends' mums which seems bizarre now, especially given that I didn't give birth to Cameron until four days before my forty-first birthday.

Mum and Dad were both strict Catholics. Marie and I attended a Catholic school, we went to Mass every Sunday, (even when we went on holiday our parents would drive around to find the local Catholic church and look up Mass times to ensure we didn't miss it). We both made our first Holy Communions at the age of seven, were taken to confession once a month and were confirmed at the age of fourteen. Catholicism was deeply ingrained in our lives, yet at that age we didn't question it. Interestingly, although Dad came from a Scottish Catholic family, he hadn't set foot inside a Catholic church for many years prior to meeting Mum. Mum, on the other hand, had been raised in the Church of England but made the decision to convert to Catholicism when she was twenty-one. Once she had made that conversion, she remained steadfast to her faith, and hence we all spent many years embarking on the journey of Catholicism with her.

Now you may ask what the connection is between religion and a travel story? The interweaving of the two will become clear soon enough.

For as long as I can remember though, our parents instilled in us a love of travel, I have vivid memories of both saying to us, "Don't marry young, go out and see the world first." As we were growing up, our parents never had the money for overseas trips, our family holidays were visits to stay with aunties, caravan holidays or touring the UK staying in youth hostels. We knew, however, that both of our parents had travelled independently before they met; Dad had been in the army and had been stationed in Aden, Germany, and Cyprus, and we knew Mum had spent two years living out in Australia.

My first glimpse of the land Down Under was through my mother's eyes. Mum had very few printed photos, the majority of her pictures having been captured onto good old-fashioned slides. How I recall the many occasions that Mum would have slide nights, either just for us as a family, or for various friends when they came to visit. Out would come the box of slides along with the screen and projector. The curtains were closed, the lights switched off, then the satisfying sound of the 'click' as the first slide dropped into place and on the big screen ahead of us Mum's black and white images of her six-week voyage and time in Australia would appear. I even remember her coming to my school when I was five or six to give a talk about Australia, accompanied with her trusty slides, and she did the same for our Brownie pack a couple of years later.

I never grew tired of watching Mum's slides or listening to the endless stories of Australia she shared. She would talk constantly about her nursing friends, the time she swam in the sea without realising the shark nets were not in place, and the joy of having barbecues on the beach on Christmas Day. We would always ask about the Sydney Opera

House, but just like its architect Jørn Utzon, Mum never had the chance to see it completed. Her only photos of this world-famous landmark showed it as an unfinished structure surrounded by scaffolding. However, the iconic bridge that stretched across Sydney Harbour always held an exceptionally special place in her heart; it was both the first and last sight she had of this city. To her it forever stood as a symbol of strength of resilience and the power of connecting people and places. I'll always remember the photo of the bridge which hung in the hallway of her home, ensuring that it too was the first and last image she saw whenever she entered or left her house. This small gesture served as a constant reminder of her deep love for the bridge and the city in which it stood.

My mum's passion for Australia had a profound impact on me. I can vividly recall feeling a deep and heartfelt connection with Sydney from as early as the age of four or five. I desperately wanted to go, yearning to see koalas, kangaroos, possums, the vibrant Blue Mountains (which I had only ever seen in black and white), and, of course, the iconic Sydney Opera House. However, little did I know that my longing would remain unfulfilled for many years. In fact, it wouldn't be until I turned forty that I would finally set foot in that wondrous country I had dreamed about for so long, and in that moment begin a brand new story of my own.

Yet for all the talking that Mum did about Australia, the endless stories she told, the hundreds of slides and pictures she showed us, little did I know then of the very big secret that she was hiding…

CHAPTER 2

"You've got a brother"

I still remember it as if it were just yesterday, I was sitting in an old armchair in the corner of our sitting room. It was October 1986, and I was fifteen. My beloved Nana (Gloria's mum) had died in February of the same year, and my grandfather had been very ill with pneumonia, so it had been a challenging few months.

The room I was sitting in was an internal room that didn't draw in a vast amount of natural light; on this occasion, it was after dark anyway, the lamp was on, and being an autumn evening, it had a cosy feel.

Mum walked in quietly and without saying a word came and sat opposite me. "Sweetheart, can we have a chat?" she asked. "Sure," I replied, thinking, "oh no, what have I done now?" but I hadn't done anything wrong; my mum Gloria was just about to make the biggest confession of her life.

"Remember how I told you I lived in Australia in my twenties?" she began. "Err, yes," I thought, "You have told me at least three hundred times, I'm sure." She continued, "When I was there, I gave birth to a baby boy; you have an older brother."

"Wait, what?" I exclaimed, suddenly sitting bolt upright. At that moment, I felt the blood drain from my body, leaving me numb and unable to speak. The only sensation I could discern was the burning of tears in my eyes, which rapidly overflowed like a burst dam, running down my cheeks in a wild torrent.

A whirlwind of emotions swirled within me, and I felt as though my body had gone into shock. We had been raised with strict religious and virtuous Catholic values from day one. Even at the age of just fifteen, I had always believed that Mum was a virgin when she married my dad.

Not only had she not been a virgin when she married, but she had given birth to another child before they met. I had a brother. Oh my God, I have a brother, I thought. I had always longed for a brother, and suddenly, I had one living on the other side of the globe. By this point, I was sobbing uncontrollably, my face contorted in a snotty, ugly cry as Mum continued to bravely share her story.

She informed me that he would be twenty-one years old by now, perhaps even having started his own family. His father, she explained, was a handsome Italian steward who had been working on the ship on which she sailed out to Australia. Their romance had blossomed during the voyage, but after he departed on the return journey, Mum discovered she was pregnant.

Alone in a foreign land on the other side of the world, with no money and no family, she found herself at the mercy of the Catholic Church, to whom she immediately turned for 'help'. The nuns with whom she made contact with in Melbourne directed her to Foundling Home for unmarried mothers in Waitara, a suburb of Northern Sydney.

This was in 1964, a time when Mum's parents back in England held very traditional values. She understood that she could never reveal her pregnancy to them, as it would not only result in her potentially being disowned by them, but would also tarnish her parents' reputation in the eyes of neighbours and friends. The gossip and judgemental attitudes of the time would have devastated her own mother, a proud and morally upright woman with strong values. It's astounding to think this was just one generation ago, yet it reflects the prevailing societal norms and attitudes of the 1960s.

Stranded far from home with no family support, minimal financial resources, and no means to provide for her baby, Mum was convinced by the nuns, under the guise of "caring" for her, that giving her child up for adoption was the only right course of action. In the circumstances she found herself in, she felt there were no other options. She was made to feel, (in the words of the nuns) a "fallen and dirty woman" who would be punished by God for her actions.

Mum delivered her baby at Mater Misericordiae Hospital in Sydney on the 9th of December 1964, a facility administered by the 'Sisters of Mercy.' She lovingly named her child Michael William Bayliss. She was later made aware that his name had been altered upon his adoption, though she remained unaware of what it had been changed to.

So, why was she choosing to reveal this to me now? Why today? It appeared that she had been wrestling with this decision for quite some time. Her own mother had passed away eight months earlier, which meant that Nana had left this world without ever knowing about the existence of her grandson. Now, Mum felt that I, at the age of fifteen, could finally be deemed "trustworthy" with this family secret, and she believed I was old enough not to accidentally let it slip to my elderly grandfather.

To this day I cannot really verbalise the tsunami of emotion that washed over me in that moment. On one hand I felt pure joy and profound love at the discovery that I had a big brother, along with an immediate desire to find and meet him. However, there was also anger and a sense of betrayal at the revelation that basically my whole life up until this moment had been a lie. I had grown up believing I was one of two children, and suddenly, I was being told I was the youngest of three.

"Does Dad know?" I asked, my voice trembling. "Yes," Mum replied, "I told him just two weeks after we met." When she shared the news with my father, his immediate response was, "well let's go out to Australia and bring him back." It was a typical reflection of my dad's compassionate, non-judgemental and open-hearted nature. Sadly, it wasn't that simple though. Michael would have been two years old by that time and already legally adopted by another family. Instead, Dad made a solemn promise to my mum: if Michael ever sought to reunite with his birth mother, my father would welcome him into our family as his own, and would provide for him in any way he might ever need or want.

Mum and Dad went on to have their big white wedding in a Catholic church in Worthing on the 30th of March 1968. Just ten months later they welcomed their "first" child, my sister Marie. I arrived twenty-one months after that. Our small family unit was then complete.

It turned out that my sister had been told about Michael when she was just eight (meaning I would have been six at that time) so everyone knew this secret except me. Everyone knew, and everyone had been living a lie. That was a very difficult and bitter pill for me to swallow. Whilst I have grown to understand why my mum hid the truth from me for so long, I admit that to this day I have an unwavering obsession with honesty and truth. I have instilled into my children that it doesn't matter what you have done or what is happening in your life, just be honest with me.

On that cold, dark October night in 1986, there was another compelling reason why Mum had chosen to finally unveil the truth to me. She had received a letter from a friend in Australia, one of the nuns whom she had maintained a friendship with all those years, and who had worked at the single mothers' home where Gloria had lived before giving birth. This friend informed Mum that there had been a recent change in Australian law, allowing birth parents to actively search for the children they had given up for adoption. Mum expressed her deep desire to find Michael but was also frightened that this quest might tear apart our own family unit. So, she asked me how I felt about her searching for him, whether I would support her in this search. "Yes, yes, of course I will, a thousand times over, yes," I exclaimed.

That night, as I went to bed with tears still in my eyes, I got down a decorative sweet jar that had been sitting on my top shelf since Christmas. I opened the lid and placed a £5 note inside; this was my weekly allowance which I had sat on my dressing table. This was the first £5 I vowed to save towards my flight to Sydney. Soon we would find my brother and promised myself I would save every single penny to get me on that flight at the first possible opportunity. I closed my eyes and I whispered, "Goodnight, Michael, soon we will be together."

CHAPTER 3

Bon Voyage

Gloria's upbringing was a very strict and traditional one. Her mother, Betty, was born in 1906, and her father, Percy, in 1910. It was a period when Great Britain was still transitioning from the Victorian era. Both of Gloria's parents grew up in the Ealing area of London. Percy, one of two children, spent a significant part of his own childhood with his grandparents in Derbyshire because his brother, Peter, had Downs syndrome and required much of their parents' attention due to his additional needs. Betty, on the other hand, was one of six daughters and, considering the era, enjoyed a relatively affluent upbringing. By all accounts, her family was fairly well-to-do.

Four out of the six sisters went on to have one child each. Dagmar had David, Edna had Pauline, Betty had Gloria, and the youngest sister, Anita, had Edward.

Percy trained and qualified as a master piano tuner with Steinway Pianos in London; however, shortly after he married Betty, they relocated from London to Worthing, where Percy found better employment opportunities. It was in Worthing that Gloria was born on 11th April 1938.

Gloria's parents held firm to their Victorian values, and as a result, she was dressed exclusively in pure white until the age of three. The spectre of World War II loomed large, and Gloria was just a year old when war broke out. Her father's significant health issues precluded him from full military service, although he did serve in the Home Guard. At the age of five, Gloria began school and received a private education, much of which was funded by her grandparents. She recognised the privilege of receiving such education during the war years, but she also detested her school experience, recalling how she felt like the "poor relation" amidst friends who had ponies and other luxuries which her parents couldn't afford.

Gloria's happiest memories of growing up were associated with her time in the St. John Ambulance Brigade, and from a young age she held a deep-seated desire to become a nurse. Her parents had other ideas for her though. Her mother was intent on raising her to follow the traditional path of previous generations – to become a dutiful wife and mother who would stay at home and "obey" her husband. From a young age, she was told they expected her to marry a doctor or a teacher, and she always said that if they could have arranged a marriage for her with their husband of choice, then they would have done so.

Indeed, this was a different era, marked by a shifting landscape for women's roles in society. After the war, more and more women were beginning to enter the workforce. However, Gloria's dreams of becoming a nurse were still initially thwarted by her parents, and instead she was compelled by them to work in a bank. She did this for three years after leaving school and loathed every second.

But by the age of nineteen, she had grown strong enough to assert her own desires and confront her parents. She was determined to follow her dream of becoming a nurse, and that's exactly what she did. She enrolled in nursing training at Worthing Hospital and worked diligently to become a State Registered Nurse, an achievement I'm pleased to say that her parents came to take immense pride in.

During her time nursing in Worthing, Gloria met and formed a strong friendship with an Australian doctor by the name of Bill Straffon. He had sailed to the UK from Melbourne, along with his wife Pam. Dr Bill became the catalyst for Gloria's dream of visiting Australia herself. When Dr Bill returned to Australia, he went out of his way to help Gloria source a nursing position in a hospital in Melbourne, even providing her with a glowing reference to assist her in securing the job.

Even with a £10 sailing ticket, it was going to take time for Gloria to save the necessary funds and complete all the required paperwork for her journey to Australia. Initially, Gloria had planned to travel to Australia with her best friend Ann, who was also a nurse. However, Ann fell in love and became engaged, which led to a change of heart about the trip. She decided to back out, and this decision came at fairly short notice.

Gloria, at the age of twenty-five, was still desperate to make the journey but understandably apprehensive about going alone. So she managed to convince her older cousin, Pauline, to accompany her. Gloria and Pauline were both only children and had spent a lot of time together during their upbringing. In many ways they were more like sisters. Their childhoods had been marked by similar upbringings, with their mothers emphasising traditional roles and expectations of becoming housewives.

Neither Gloria nor Pauline was content with that path though, being determined to explore the world beyond, so they embarked on the process of applying for tickets, visas, and all the necessary arrangements for their journey to Australia.

It's easy to forget that in 1963-4 the digital world we know today did not exist. There was no internet to Google pictures or read reviews of their destination, and no travel agents on the high street where they could drop in to pick up glossy brochures. Even in 1963 Gloria's parents didn't own a television set. So, when Gloria made the decision to travel to Australia with Pauline, they truly were sailing into the unknown, committing themselves to a minimum of two years there. This was the condition of their £10 ticket: they had to agree to two years of work in Australia or else they would have to pay for their return fare, which, from what I understand, was around £300 – a significant increase from the £10 they initially paid.

On February 5th 1964, the day finally arrived for Gloria and Pauline to depart. Their lives were packed into two trucks, and they were bound for Southampton. Since neither Gloria's nor Pauline's parents owned a car, a taxi transported them all to Southampton docks from Worthing. Emotional farewells were exchanged, and tears were shed. Then the two girls boarded the ship and found their cabin, marking the beginning of their extraordinary adventure.

Their ship, the *Castel Felice*, translated as the "Happy Castle," belonged to the Italian Sitmar line. Between 1952 and 1970, this ship undertook an astonishing 101 voyages between England and Australasia, carrying 100,000 immigrants to Australia and New Zealand. It was a far cry from the luxurious cruise ships we know today, but this modest vessel was to be Gloria and Pauline's home for the next five weeks.

Their sleeping quarters were a small inside cabin with four bunks and no toilet, only a sink. Even married couples were to be separated on this voyage, and Gloria and Pauline shared their cabin with a married woman, while her husband occupied a similar cabin in the men's quarters.

As Gloria and Pauline's parents stood heartbroken on the docks, the *Castel Felice* sounded her horn and began her journey down Southampton's waters towards the English Channel. Excited passengers cheered and waved their farewells. The ship made her way to the open waters until she became a mere speck on the horizon. Gloria and Pauline were en route to Australia; their incredible voyage had begun.

'Gloria's parents, Percy & Betty'.

Pauline (left), Gloria (2nd left) with new friends they
made on the ship during their voyage to Australia.

CHAPTER 4

A Baby is Born

A s the small ship *Castel Felice* embarked on its journey southward, it charted a course through the Bay of Biscay, traversed the Mediterranean, and finally anchored in Port Said. Continuing through the Suez Canal, it made a pit stop in Aden. (Little did Gloria realise at the time that Bill, her one-day future husband, was stationed in Aden with the Royal Engineers. Their own story, however, was still a few years away in the making.)

Amid the voyage, many passengers succumbed to seasickness, confining themselves to their cabins. In stark contrast, Gloria quickly discovered her remarkable sea legs – a trait that, fortunately, has been passed down to both me and my own children. With only a handful of passengers wandering the ship or attending meals in the dining room, Gloria took the opportunity to socialise and forge new friendships, something which had always been very natural for her.

Gloria, a captivating young woman with fiery red hair, quickly became the recipient of affection from a middle-aged gentleman named Joe. However, Gloria's eyes were already very much set on a handsome Italian dining room steward by the name of Gabriele Scordamaglia.

Pauline shared with me how Gloria had a habit of slipping out of their cabin at night, under the guise of needing to use the bathroom. She would be absent for extended periods, leading to the assumption that these late-night escapades were, in fact, secret rendezvous with Gabriele in the ship's broom cupboard!

Gloria was relishing her new-found freedom and the opportunity to break away from her overly controlling parents. Pauline, on the other hand, was not only suffering with seasickness but also homesickness. She had recently met her future husband, David, at their cousin Edward's birthday party in the November prior to their departure. It became evident to both of them that they harboured strong feelings for one other. In fact, David had tearfully pleaded with Pauline not to leave when he called her to say his goodbyes before she sailed. She was torn between her love for David and her commitment to Gloria, not wanting to let her down.

During the voyage, a tender romance blossomed between Gabriele and Gloria, a few stolen moments and a few stolen kisses. However, they both understood from the outset that their love was possibly destined to be short-lived. Gloria was set to stay in Australia, while Gabriele would almost immediately embark on the return journey.

After a five-week journey at sea, the Castel Felice finally arrived in Melbourne, where Gloria and Pauline were to disembark. Gloria had already secured a job at Heidelberg Hospital in St Kilda, and arrangements had been made for transportation to pick them up from the docks. Gloria was the first to be taken to the hospital, and then Pauline was driven to her accommodation in a separate part of the city.

However, as soon as Gloria settled into her nursing quarters, she couldn't resist the urge to sneak out again. She immediately headed back to the docks to spend her very first night in Australia in a hotel with Gabriele. The following morning, Gabriele returned to the ship for its journey back to Europe. He promised to see Gloria again on his next voyage to Melbourne, but as the ship sailed back out to sea, it marked the last time Gloria would ever see or hear from him.

Gloria quickly had a new love though – Australia. The feeling of finding a place she could call home was instantaneous, marking the beginning of a deep and enduring affection for the nation which she cherished her entire life. She adored the country, the climate, her new job, and the people she encountered, whether that was through her work in the hospital or the Catholic church she promptly started attending. She had never been happier.

In contrast, Pauline's feelings were mixed. While she had some fondness for Australia, her heart yearned for David. Almost immediately upon their arrival, she began planning her return to England. However, this process required saving up for the ticket and once again navigating the necessary paperwork. Despite Pauline's preparations to go back home, she and Gloria still cherished a few joyful weeks together in Melbourne. They ventured to Healesville Zoo, attended a performance of The Mikado, and even caught a glimpse of the Beatles on the balcony of a local hotel.

Then, almost overnight, life took a dramatic turn for Gloria when she discovered that she was pregnant. Gabriele had sailed into the sunset, and despite Gloria's numerous attempts to contact him through letters to share the news, she received no response.

Terrified, overwhelmed and unsure of what to do or who to turn to, Gloria found herself in a difficult predicament. Her very Victorian upbringing ruled out the possibility of returning to England or telling her parents. Her devout Catholic beliefs immediately ruled out the option of termination. With no close friends to turn to, the long distance and the time delay of five to six weeks for mail to reach home, and the high cost of pre-booked phone calls to England, which she couldn't afford, Gloria had never felt so scared, isolated, and alone. All she was certain of was her determination to do the very best for the little life growing inside her.

Gloria eventually confided in Pauline, but by then Pauline had already booked her passage back to England. Feeling desperate, Gloria turned to the only other person she believed she could trust, her parish priest, Father Burns. He promised Gloria that the church would take care of everything, and arrangements were made for her to leave Melbourne and move to Waitara in New South Wales. The Waitara Foundling Home, established in 1898 by the Sisters of Mercy in Northern Sydney, served as a sanctuary for babies and unmarried mothers. Before leaving Melbourne, Gloria purchased a wedding ring to conceal her status as an unmarried mother. She gave up the job she loved, bade goodbye to Pauline and embarked on what she described as her "journey of shame" to Sydney.

In June 1964, now aged twenty-six, Gloria arrived at Waitara, where her accommodations were rudimentary at best. She found herself in what was equivalent to a metal-framed hospital bed in a shared dormitory with around twenty other pregnant girls and women, ranging in age from young teenagers to those in their early forties. The Sisters of Mercy who oversaw the facility weren't overtly cruel, as they provided for their basic needs. However, from the very first day, it was made abundantly clear by the nuns that in the eyes of God, Gloria's 'sins' were "equated with those of a murderer". These were the exact words which had been spoken to her.

For so long, Gloria had dreamed of what her life in Australia would be like, but the reality was now starkly different from what she had envisioned.

Now, at the time of writing this, I have a twenty-six-year-old daughter of my own. As a mother I find it impossible to comprehend the idea of her enduring a situation like the one my own mum faced, all alone on the opposite side of the world, with me as a parent unaware or unable to provide help and support. As I grow older, the profound isolation, judgement and despair Gloria experienced whilst pregnant becomes increasingly horrific to me.

During her pregnancy, Gloria grappled with severe back pain and was granted permission to attend a weekly physiotherapy appointment. She was transported there and back each week by the same woman, Sylvia. Sylvia became the first person to truly show her real empathy, and although just a few years older than Gloria, Sylvia quickly became the mother figure that Gloria desperately needed at that time, and they formed a friendship which would endure throughout their whole lives.

The following months at Waitara proved to be exceptionally challenging for Gloria. She experienced an increasing sense of desperation and loneliness. Each day, she keenly felt her child growing inside her, sensing its initial kicks and every twist and turn. However, she had no one to share these important milestones with, no parental support, no siblings, no husband to snuggle up to at night, to place his hand on her belly, to partake in the excitement, no one to reassure her that everything would be alright. Most nights, Gloria silently cried herself to sleep as she lay on her small, uncomfortable bed, cradling her growing bump, adoring her baby, and wishing desperately that she was able to give them the life they both deserved.

On the 9th of December 1964, after more than five months of living in Waitara, Gloria was transferred to the Mater Misericordiae Hospital, where she gave birth to her baby, a little boy. He was perfect in every way. She particularly noticed his beautiful eyelashes and teeny, tiny fingernails. Gloria named her newborn son Michael William. Unlike Gloria who had fair skin and red hair, Michael inherited his father's Italian genes, with olive skin, a head of thick brown hair, and big brown eyes.

The nuns wanted to take Michael from Gloria immediately, but she adamantly fought to keep him by her side until the time would come when he was found an adoptive family. She was determined he was not going to be alone for one minute. For the first ten days of his life, she cradled him, fed him, telling him day and night how much she loved him and always would. She whispered to him how their love would endure forever but that his new Mummy and Daddy would be able to provide him with so much more than she ever could. She emphasised how he would now be able grow up with his head held high, instead of becoming the innocent victim of other people's judgment and gossip.

Within a matter of days, the nuns informed Gloria that they had found an adoptive family for Michael. Though she didn't know many details, she did learn that he was being placed with a caring Catholic family, something which held great importance for her. This family, residing within the Blue Mountains area, had previous experience with adoption and had already welcomed two other children into their family. Gloria took comfort from the fact that her son would immediately have adoring siblings as well as loving parents.

To Gloria, this adoptive family sounded as close to perfect as any prospective family could be. Despite the heart-breaking decision to give up her beloved baby, she believed that this family could provide

her beautiful son with the life he deserved – a
him herself but was neither able to, nor allo

After ten unforgettable and cherished ⟨
told by the nuns that Michael's adoptive fai
him to his new home. She washed and dres
swaddled him in his shawl; she held him close fo.
whispering a lifetime of loving wishes, then kissed his tiny n.
With tears streaming down her cheeks and her heart ripped in.
million pieces, Gloria said her agonising farewell. One of the waiting
nuns then took Michael from her arms. As he went off to start his new
life, Gloria sent with him a christening gown and a Bible that she had
chosen for him, with the deepest hope that one day he would receive
these items from his adoptive family and learn just how deeply his
birth mother had loved and treasured him.

Gloria had already signed the adoption paperwork a few days earlier
under the watchful supervision of the Mother Superior. It was yet
another occasion where she was degraded and humiliated for her
perceived 'sins'. She always recalled how the Mother Superior left her
under no doubt that she would never see, nor have any contact with
Michael ever again, and nor should she ever make any attempt to.

With Michael now taken from her arms, it was Sylvia, her steadfast
friend, who picked Gloria up from the Foundling Home and brought
her back to live with her own family. This included Sylvia's husband,
also named Michael, and their two grown-up sons.

Gloria, with hormones still surging through her body and grief
tearing her heart apart, felt like she was screaming internally but was
so numb that she could no longer physically cry. Her only comfort
during this time was knowing that baby Michael would be in his new
home and in the arms of his loving adopted family in time for his first
Christmas... or rather, this was what the nuns led her to believe.

CHAPTER 5

Returning to England

Michael was now officially adopted, and Gloria's baby boy was gone forever from her arms, but never from her heart. She had to get on with life though, she had to survive. She found another nursing job at a hospital in Sydney and spent the remaining time of her two years in Australia working there. She loved life in Sydney but every day she thought about Michael and prayed for him. Endless wonderings filled her mind: has he cut his first tooth yet? Has he taken his first steps? The knowledge that another woman was witnessing these milestones, not her, was deeply painful and played like a heart-wrenching show reel in her mind day after day. She physically ached with sorrow as she visualised him running up to another woman with outstretched arms, calling for his "Mummy," or knowing she couldn't be there to soothe him when he was sick.

Each and every day Gloria's heart yearned for her little boy, but she masked her sorrow with a smile as she attempted to get on with life and find her new normal. She confided in Sylvia about her grief for Michael, but to everyone else in her life, he remained hidden and unknown.

Gloria formed numerous lasting friendships in Australia, relationships she would cherish throughout her lifetime. These friends became her pen pals and Christmas card exchange companions for many years to come.

In what seemed no time at all, Gloria's contracted two-year stay in Australia was up. Did she want to return to England? No. But did she feel an obligation to go home and see her parents? Yes.

So once more, Gloria boarded a ship, preparing for the six-week voyage back to England. As the ship set sail from Sydney, she recalled sobbing constantly for three consecutive days as the ship sailed down to New Zealand to pick up more returning immigrants.

Two years earlier when Gloria had embarked on her journey out to Australia, she sailed through the Mediterranean Sea, the Suez Canal, and the Indian Ocean. Her return voyage took her across the Pacific Ocean, through the Panama Canal, and eventually across the Atlantic. By the time she reached Southampton again, she had completed a full circumnavigation of the globe by ship, making stops at various countries along the way to enable the vessel to restock their supplies of food and fuel.

Pauline fondly recalls going to Southampton to meet Gloria from the ship, along with Gloria's excited parents, Betty and Percy. She remembered Gloria getting off the ship looking slightly the worse for wear. Since Gloria wasn't known for heavy drinking, one could only imagine that this was a last-ditch attempt to numb the pain of returning and leaving her now seventeen-month-old son on the other side of the world.

By this time, Pauline had happily married David, reuniting with him in September 1964 after her return from Australia. During those two years, she and Gloria hadn't spoken in person, mainly due to the high cost of phone calls. In fact, in all that time Gloria had only managed two brief three-minute phone calls with her parents, both of which had to be pre-booked and took place on Christmas Day.

Pauline naturally had a multitude of questions she longed to ask Gloria on their reunion, but of course, they couldn't discuss Michael in front of Gloria's parents. They all took a taxi together for the fifty-mile trip back to Sussex, and by the time Pauline returned home to David, the subject of Michael had not been broached.

The moment Gloria reached her hometown of Worthing, she knew precisely what she wanted and needed to do: book a passage for her return to Australia, only this time she booked a one-way ticket. She had not only left her son in Australia, but a big part of her heart as well. She was going to return once more to the land she now called home and settle there for life.

However, her immediate return wasn't possible; she needed to save up for the fare, and negotiate embassies and visas yet again, so it would be about another year before she could set off. Gloria felt suffocated in Worthing though, so she found employment at a hospital in Ashford, near Heathrow Airport, and shared an apartment with some of her nursing colleagues.

In January 1967 one of Gloria's flatmates, an Australian, was preparing to return to her homeland and invited Gloria to her farewell party. However, by the time the party rolled around, Gloria had just completed a long shift at the hospital and wasn't in the mood to party. She tried to make excuses to get out of going, but her friend wasn't accepting no for an answer. So, reluctantly, Gloria agreed to go, telling herself it would be just for one drink.

True to her word, Gloria had just one drink at the party, itching to make her exit. She slipped out quietly and was on her way down the staircase when a rugged Scotsman enquired, "Hey, where do you think you're escaping to this early?" Gloria explained her fatigue and her lack of enthusiasm for the party, but the Scotsman, persistent in his pursuit, introduced himself as Bill and mentioned that it was his birthday the next day and immediately invited her to go out for a birthday drink with him.

The following evening, January 8th, Gloria and Bill went out for their first drink together, although they didn't openly label it as a date. Gloria candidly told Bill how she was tired of friends trying to set her up with guys and made sure he was fully aware that she had a one-way ticket booked to Australia. Bill, in response, shared that he had recently left the army and was thoroughly enjoying his carefree, single life. Despite their initial agreement to have a "no-strings-attached" friendship, to quite simply hang out and share some fun times together, little did they know that Cupid had just shot a golden arrow through their hearts. Within days, these two individuals who had been determined to remain footloose and fancy free had fallen head over heels in love, and just two weeks later, Bill proposed to Gloria.

Gloria had no hesitation in saying "yes", but she also knew it was time to reveal her past and tell Bill about Michael. As mentioned earlier, Bill's reaction was a simple, "Let's go and get him, and I'll raise him as my own." Gloria desperately wished that this was feasible, but Michael had been adopted for two years by now, so the possibility wasn't even an option.

There was one more big hurdle standing between them, Bill did not want to live in Australia. Gloria had a huge choice to make, but so deep was her love for Bill that her one-way ticket to Australia went unused, and instead they found themselves planning a wedding just fourteen months later.

A wedding, a new home and two daughters later, Gloria fronted an image of being a mother of two, but in her heart she was always a mother to three. We didn't know this or even notice it at the time but apparently every year on December 9th (Michael's birthday) she would make her excuses for going out and would make her way down to our local Catholic church where she would light a candle for him.

During the early years of their marriage Gloria and Bill had a significant mortgage on their first home so money was tight. Family holidays in the UK were the most basic, yet always joyful. As a family, we had next to nothing in terms of material wealth yet lacked for nothing in happiness. Our parents showered us with love, but never in a way which felt suffocating.

The dynamics of overseas travel were also turned on their head during this time too. Sea voyages, which had once been the more affordable option, were now largely replaced by cruises, and had largely become a luxury enjoyed by the most affluent. Air travel, on the other hand, had become the more cost-effective and convenient option. The problem was that Gloria and Bill's finances couldn't accommodate either option. Moreover, Bill had a deep-seated fear of flying. This fear had its roots in a traumatic event where he witnessed an army aircraft, carrying many of his friends, taking off and then crashing back down on its tail directly in front of him, erupting into a devastating fireball. The experience left him helplessly watching as his friends and comrades perished in the blazing wreckage. Understandably, he swore that day that he would never fly again.

Gloria's heart yearned every day to return to Australia, but obstacle after obstacle seem to stand in her way.

Her marriage and commitment to Bill was unwavering though. They faced numerous ups and downs over the years, challenges that might have torn apart many younger couples. Yet they hailed from a generation that believed in fixing things rather than discarding them. They worked tirelessly to ensure the success of their marriage. As they overcame the early challenges, they only grew closer and closer as the years passed, honouring their marriage vow of "till death us do part" with deep devotion and commitment.

Years went by, and there were no significant developments in this part of the story until that fateful night in October 1986 when Mum told me I had a brother. Although she had told my sister several years earlier, my sister had never felt any desire to find or know our brother.

In contrast, I became completely obsessed by the idea. In the following weeks and months that passed in 1986/87, I held on to the hope that it was only a matter of time; Mum would find Michael, we would experience a joyful reunion filled with hugs, kisses and happy tears, all living happily ever after. But just a few months later Mum delivered another bombshell: she had changed her mind about searching for Michael.

CHAPTER 6

Finding Michael

It was in the spring of 1987 when Mum dropped that second bombshell. After many months of soul-searching and several letters exchanged with parties in Australia, she had come to a decision – she was not going to actively search for Michael. To this day, I still wonder who those letters were exchanged with and exactly what was discussed. Could it have been correspondence with the Sisters of Mercy at Waitara, and if so, what exactly transpired in that correspondence?

I remembered what Mum had told me the year before; Mother Superior had sternly informed her that she would never see Michael again, nor should she ever try to. Had she made contact with the nuns, and once again been riddled with guilt for her so-called sins, and reminded of her punishment from God?

Once again I found myself sobbing and fervently pleading with her to look for him. In response, she gently said, "Darling, he might not even be aware that he was adopted," and then added, "or he may know and simply have no desire to have contact with me." It was years later that I came to understand that a significant fear was the possibility of being rejected by him. With tears in her eyes and an expression of complete helplessness, she softly said, "Who am I to suddenly reappear in his life when another family has spent twenty-two years raising him? I don't want to disrupt his life now. I love him far too much for that."

I understood her decision, but I was still utterly heartbroken by it. I was desperate to find my brother, and it felt as though the ground had been pulled out from under me.

What Gloria had discovered, however, was the existence of a central reunion register in Australia. This register allowed her to leave a letter and her contact information so that if Michael ever wished to find her, he could do so immediately. We both hoped that he too would use this register and make contact with his birth mother sooner rather than later.

More than two years passed, with absolutely no news from Australia, and by this I was now eighteen years old. I brought up the topic of searching for him once again with Mum, but I received a similar response. "My details are on the register, so if he wants to find me, he can do so right away. I suppose he either doesn't know he's adopted, or he doesn't want any contact with me," she said with a defeated look. She was convinced it was the latter though because when she was initially told about his adoptive family, she was informed that they already had other adopted children, and that Michael would always be raised knowing the truth.

At eighteen I was an adult myself now and without any further discussion with my mum I made the decision to begin searching for Michael, but I was faced with the daunting question, where on earth do I start? This was still the 1980s, several years before anyone even had a mobile phone, let alone access to email and the internet.

The only organisation I was aware of that helped in such searches was the Salvation Army, and I knew they had a branch in Worthing, the neighbouring town to where we lived. I chose to write them a letter. It took a few weeks for them to respond, and when they did, they provided me with information about a central office, which, to the best of my memory, was in London. I sent another letter to this central office, but this time it took them even longer to reply, although they were very helpful. However, there was a significant hurdle: as his sister, I was not able to access Michael's adoption records. Only his birth mother could do that, and I would only inherit that right after her death. Without access to the adoption records, I had no idea what his name had been changed to when he was adopted, and I therefore had no idea of the name of the person I should be searching for. I had hit a brick wall.

Further years passed and I entered my twenties, I still longed to fulfil my earliest childhood dream of visiting Australia, but I couldn't bring myself to do it. Michael could be anywhere, and I wouldn't recognise him. I knew I'd find myself staring at every man of a certain age with slightly olive skin and brown eyes, wondering, could you be my brother? He might serve me in a restaurant, or I might sit next to him on the bus and never realise it.

I was self-aware enough even then to recognise that such a trip could take a toll on my mental health. So I made myself a promise that my first journey to Australia would be to meet Michael one day. I often daydreamed about that moment – walking out of the arrivals hall in Sydney airport, scanning the waiting crowds for his face, and then falling into one another's arms, shedding tears of happiness.

I even reached out to the British TV show Surprise Surprise to try to find him, but I never received a response from them. Perhaps their researchers understood that Mum would need to sign the papers to access his adoption records, making my efforts futile.

By the time I reached my late twenties, I had not only matured significantly but had also become a parent myself, giving my parents their first grandchild. This experience brought me even closer to my mum and gave me a deeper understanding of the emotions she must have felt when she had to give her own baby away at just ten days old. As a mother, the thought of such a situation made me feel sick to the core. I know Mum often wondered if Michael had a family of his own by now. He would be well into his thirties, and there was a strong possibility that he might have children. My mum, now in her sixties, was aware of her time clock ticking away but had come to terms with the idea that, despite her being on the Australian reunion register for well over a decade, Michael just didn't want to have contact with her. She expressed her relief that she hoped this meant that it was because he was happy in his life and with his adoptive family, but as much as she tried to hide it, I always connected with the internal pain she was feeling and how desperately she wanted to have contact with him. So many years had passed, yet her love for him had never ever faded.

As I reached my thirties, technology was rapidly advancing. We had the internet, Google search engines and the like. I began spending hours searching for information with his birth name, Mum's maiden name, and Australian adoption details, but alas, all these searches brought forward nothing.

Around the age of thirty-five, I discovered a new website called Oz Reunion, which aimed to reunite long-lost or adopted family members in Australia. Once again, I pored over that website for hours, hoping that Michael had already posted something there. Perhaps he didn't even know his birth name and was searching with his adopted name, which we didn't know. So, night after night, I went through every person on that website, but my search was fruitless.

I did, however, register my own details on the website and created a search looking for my brother, Michael William Bayliss, born in Sydney on December 9, 1964, with a little background information and an assurance of how much he was loved and still wanted by both his birth mother and me. I checked back to the site frequently, but there was never any response.

Then, around eighteen months later, an email popped into my inbox from the Oz Reunion website with the heading 're Michael William Bayliss.' My heart immediately started pounding as I clicked frantically on the keyboard to open it. Was this from my brother? After all these years of longing, dreaming, and waiting, had he finally made contact?

Alas, to my slight disappointment, it was not from my Michael himself, but rather from a researcher of an Australian television series called Find My Family. The researcher, named Helen, asked if I would like them to help me search for my brother? Of course I leaped at this opportunity, typing my response so quickly I'm amazed the keyboard didn't go up in smoke. These people were reunion specialists, they were doing this work every day, and they would know exactly how and where to look. After twenty-two years of searching, I finally had some real hope. Mum by this time was just a few months away from her seventieth birthday; what an incredible surprise it would be for her if I could find him in time for her special day. My mind immediately went into overdrive with the excitement and anticipation.

I sent back all the information I had, which was fairly limited but hopefully enough for them to make a start. But alas, a couple of weeks later, the researcher came back to me again. "In order for us to access your brother's adoption records, we need your mother Gloria to sign the attached authorisation papers." We were back to square one. By this stage, I was so desperate that if it hadn't been for the fact her signature needed witnessing, I would have forged it (after all, I had become quite an expert at that in my teen years, writing letters to my teachers to get out of PE!) Instead of forgery though, I did the right thing and spoke to Mum, telling her how this TV company had been in touch with me and offered help to find Michael.

Her standard response was again the one that I had heard so many times over the years. "All my details are on the Australian register; if he wants to find me, he can do so straight away. He obviously doesn't want to find me." "Pleeeeeease, Mum," I begged her. "This is the best chance we've ever had."

With Mum approaching seventy I think the realisation was setting in that she wasn't getting any younger. I knew her heart still yearned for her baby boy as much then, by now forty-two years later, as it did the day she had to give him up. I knew she also had the eternal question going around in her mind as to whether she now had other grandchildren as well.

"Send me the papers, I'll sign them," she finally said. The sense of elation I felt was electrifying. At last, we could move forward. The forms were duly signed, witnessed, and emailed to the researcher in Australia.

It was just a matter of days when I received an email from a different researcher, Dominique, which read, "Just to give you an update, we have now accessed your mother's adoption records, and we can begin searching for your brother." I was elated beyond words, I don't think either Mum or I had expected such fast progress, so I decided not to tell Mum immediately, hoping that perhaps I could still surprise her on her seventieth birthday when they found him.

It was less than a week later, on February 26, 2008, when I came back from doing the morning school run with my daughter to find a message on the main answering machine at home. I listened as a man with a strong Australian accent spoke, "Oh hi, this is Greg from Network Seven television in Australia, we are the production company for Find my Family. I have some news I want to share with you. It's late here in Sydney now, though, so I'll try and call you back in the morning."

Again, my heart was racing, and I wanted to call him back immediately, except 1) he didn't leave his number, and 2) he was probably tucked up in his bed right now. All day my head was spinning; have they found him? Does he want to meet me? It must have been one of the longest days of my life. I worked late in the study that night, willing the phone to ring, my hand quite literally hovering over the receiver all evening. It was close to midnight when finally the telephone on the desk next to me rang. I picked it up in a split second. "Hello, is that Terri?" the Australian voice on the other end enquired. "Yes, yes it is," I replied, with my heart pounding. He continued, "Terri, hi. This is Greg, and I am the director of Network Seven. I am sorry to call you so late in the UK, but let me assure you that if you were not on the other side of the world, I would be on your doorstep right now and not on the phone to you..."

I listened intently for the next few minutes as he continued his message. As he spoke my heart sank and I felt my entire body freeze, as if time had just stood still. I put the phone down in stony silence, knowing in that moment our lives had changed forever.

Michael was dead.

Greg told me little else at that time, other than they had discovered Michael had died in America in 2003. He did know he was adopted, and he did want to find his birth mother. In fact, he had flown from

Australia to the UK a few years earlier in an attempt to find her. He had spent virtually all of his adult life searching for her and had even added his details to exactly the same register that Mum was on. For some reason, they had never been matched.

I was numb, completely broken. I felt like someone had reached in and ripped my heart from my chest. All those years searching for him, and all the time he was also searching for his mum. How could this possibly have happened? How could the register not have matched them? I cried and I wailed like I had never cried before. How was I ever going to get over this? And worst of all, how was I ever going to break this news to Gloria?

CHAPTER 7

Michael becomes Mark...

The phone call I received from Greg at Network Seven in Australia left me utterly distraught, not just for myself but more so for Mum. Having received Greg's phone call just before midnight, I spent the entire night sobbing uncontrollably like I had never sobbed before or since. As a funeral celebrant, I had shouldered the grief of others for many years, offering words like "cherish the memories, remember the good times," yet in this moment, I had no memories, no good times to recall, just shattered dreams and the knowledge that I had to break my mum's heart all over again. I have dozens of books about grief and bereavement and yet not one spoke of how you even begin to grieve for someone you've never met, but someone you've dreamed about and longed to meet for so many years? (Twenty-two years for me, an agonising forty-two years for Gloria.)

By then, I had been working as a funeral celebrant for just over five years, and I had to go and conduct a funeral the following day at 10 a.m. for a gentleman I had been working alongside as he battled a terminal illness. I was determined to honour my promise to him and ensure he had the fabulous send-off that he and I had meticulously planned together. To this day, I still don't know how I managed it. I cried all the way to the crematorium, sat in the car park and reapplied my makeup, maintained a professional demeanour throughout the ceremony, and then cried all the way back home. I cried and I cried, and I cried some more, I honestly believed that there was no way I would ever even begin to heal from this.

I still had a million questions racing through my mind, questions that had been overshadowed by the shock and numbness during my conversation with Greg the previous night. I couldn't simply accept the revelation of "he died in America in 2003" and leave it at that. So, I promptly sent an email back to the researcher I had been in contact with, seeking more details about Michael. How had they learned of his passing? Had they spoken to a family member? What were the circumstances of his death? Was he buried somewhere, and if so, where could I find his grave? Who and what was Michael? What was his life like? And, of course the question that had weighed so heavily on my mother's heart for all those years: did he have any children? Did Gloria have more grandchildren? I hoped with all my heart that if he did then that might just be some tiny solace amid such tragic news.

The next day, Dominique, the researcher, called me from Australia. She told me that at the time of his adoption, Michael's name had been changed to Mark.

(From this point onwards I am going to use an alias for Mark's surname, along with the first names of his adoptive family, as I am not able to obtain their permission to include their true identity in this story.)

The adoption records showed that he had been adopted by the Stockbridge family, and his name was changed from Michael William Bayliss to Mark Christopher Stockbridge.

Once the researchers had a name to work with, 'Mark Stockbridge,' they scoured the Sydney telephone directory for any listings related to M. Stockbridge. On one call answered by a woman, the lady responded to the researcher's enquiry, saying, "I am not 'the' M. Stockbridge you are looking for, but I know who you are talking about – that is my brother Mark, who passed away five years ago. I am his younger sister, Melanie."

Upon receiving my email, Dominique promptly reached out to Melanie and came back to me with additional information. She shared that Mark was a teacher, a very popular one at that, known for his good looks and a wide circle of friends. She added that Mark had a passion for singing, and he had never married or had any children. She also told me that Mark's adoptive mother was still alive, but their father had passed away when they were children.

That was all the information available in that call, a modest but vital start to piecing together the many, many parts to this puzzle.

In response, I composed another email to Australia, this time addressing it to Melanie and her mother. I conveyed my deepest sorrow for their loss, provided a brief insight into Gloria's story and my long-standing quest to find my brother. I expressed how much I would be open to establishing contact with them if they were willing, and I included all my contact details. I asked Dominique if she would pass this letter on to the family, which she willingly agreed to do.

Simultaneously I grappled with the daunting task of breaking the devastating news to Mum. There was a part of me contemplating the idea of concealing the truth. I thought to myself, perhaps I could just tell her they couldn't trace him and spare her the pain. Yet, I was also acutely aware of the pain she was already carrying, and as someone who is obsessively committed to the truth, I knew I could never carry it off anyway.

My parents' ruby (fortieth) wedding anniversary was exactly a month away, followed by my mother's seventieth birthday a mere eleven days later. We had grand celebrations planned for both occasions. Initially, I contemplated waiting until after these events to break the heart-breaking news, not wanting in any way to spoil these joyous family moments for her. However, this would mean keeping the truth concealed from her for another six weeks, and deep down, I knew I couldn't do it. Each time I opened my mouth, tears welled up, and my phone conversations with Mum, which generally took place every two to three days, now almost always included her asking, "Any news from Australia yet?" I knew I just couldn't possibly live a lie with her for the next six weeks. I had so desperately wanted to reunite her with her son in time for her seventieth birthday, and now instead I was trying to plan how I was going to break it to her that her son was dead. It was a sickening feeling, but in my heart I knew I needed to tell her the truth as soon as possible, face to face. The challenge was that she lived over two hundred miles away.

Despite this emotional turmoil, I still had three days of funerals booked in for the rest of that week and, committed to my work and the bereaved families I serve, I had to honour those. I pushed myself through those services, delivering each ceremony with my customary professionalism and grace, determined not to let the excruciating pain and raw grief seep through that I was feeling myself, even though I felt like it was oozing out of every pore. I was fortunate to have some incredibly supportive friends and my immediate family, who virtually carried me through that week. Without their unwavering support, I'm certain I would not have survived without breaking down completely.

During those three days, I also intentionally let Mum's calls go to voicemail, because it was far easier to avoid speaking to her than having to fabricate a lie.

Then the day arrived when I had to embark on the 230-mile journey from Sussex to Wales. My first stop was at the flower shop, where I had arranged for their florist to create a large bouquet of flowers for me. The bouquet featured reds, whites, and blues to mirror the colours of the Australian flag, and included some Australian eucalyptus and white orchids, two of Gloria's favourite flowers.

The road to my parents' home was always a slow and winding one, typically taking around five hours. I remember that day as if it were yesterday, I could barely see the road through my tears, and it rained incessantly throughout the entire journey, as if the angels themselves wept with me.

Even though I had made this journey countless times before, I kept the satnav on, not so much for navigation but as a way to track the time, and on this occasion, the time-to-destination clock felt like a ticking time bomb: three hours until I break my mum's heart – two hours until I break my mum's heart. I recall stopping briefly once for a toilet break and receiving a heartfelt text from my dear friend Marian (who has since passed away). Her message read, "I am right with you, I'm hugging you tightly and holding your Mum's hand." Even writing those words now brings tears to my eyes, but they provided me with so much strength at that critical moment.

Finally, I arrived at my parents' house in Wales. I left the bouquet of flowers in the car to avoid arousing any suspicion, and walked through the front door. This was the first time I had ever visited them without calling and making plans first, and, as expected, they were overjoyed by what they thought was a "lovely surprise visit." Fortunately, a quick touch-up of makeup down the road had concealed my red, puffy eyes. As soon as I set eyes on Mum I instantly felt my tears welling up again, and I fought like mad to hold them back.

Mum immediately went into full 'faffing' mode, asking, "do you want a coffee, darling? Are you going to stay the night? I must go and make up the spare bed, sorry the house is such a mess" (said whilst shuffling newspapers and magazines). Inside, I wanted to shout, "Please, just sit down and be still!" but of course, I didn't utter those words. Instead, I allowed her to prepare the coffee and complete her fussing before she finally sat down beside me and asked, "So, what brings us the pleasure of this unexpected visit, and why didn't you ring first?"

I knew I couldn't delay the news a moment longer, and no matter how hard I tried, I couldn't hold back the tears. I reached over, gently took her hand, and said, "The TV company in Australia managed to make a breakthrough to find Michael, but I'm so, so sorry, Mum, he died five years ago."

I watched in what felt like slow motion as every drop of colour drained from her face, and in the background I heard my dad let out a deep, sorrowful groan. I could tell Mum was in shock and I just wanted to take the pain away from her; she didn't cry in the immediate instance, instead she leaned over and held me tightly me as by now I couldn't control the tears streaming down my cheeks. She cradled me and kissed my forehead and whispered softly, "My little baby – I feel like I have lost him all over again."

If I had to pinpoint the single worst day of my life, that day would undoubtedly be it. Looking back as a fifty-three-year-old writing this book, I wonder if thirty-seven-year-old me could have handled it better? I live with that memory and the emotion of that moment every single day. I can still vividly recall the look of loss and excruciation in Gloria's eyes as I shared the limited information I had. "Michael did want to find you, Mum. All those years you believed he didn't want to know you, but he did, he was actively searching for you. He was on the same register as you in Australia, but for some reason you were never matched."

"I should have searched for him," she said, her voice heavy with regret. "He went to his grave thinking I didn't want to know him, when I did. You know, I never stopped loving him or thinking of him, not for one day." "He knows that now, Mum. I'm sure of it," I reassured her while still clasping her cold trembling hand.

We talked and talked, all evening, all night and well into the early hours. Just as I predicted, she asked me very early on in the conversation, "do you know whether he had children?" and when I replied that he didn't, I knew that was yet another loss to her. Neither of us could comprehend how the reunion register had failed to connect them, Mum had always been assured, "if your son wants to make contact with you, then he could do so immediately". It would take another three years before this mystery was finally unravelled, but let me just say that the Catholic nuns played a big part in it.

I explained to Mum that I had sent an email to Michael/Mark's adoptive mum and sister, including all my contact information, but as yet I hadn't received any response. It was very early days, but Mum had so many questions: "how did he die? Where did he die? Was he buried and if so where was his final resting place? Was anybody with him when he died?" Those along with a million and one other questions were still unanswered. "Try to be patient, Mum," I said reassuringly, "it's very early days and I am sure we will hear more from his family soon."

Just four weeks later, we celebrated Mum and Dad's ruby wedding anniversary as best as we could, wearing smiles on the outside while grappling with deep grief within. Afterwards, I treated all of us to a holiday in Devon; there were five of us, me and my parents, my daughter Georgia who was ten at the time, and my sister, Marie. We all did our very best to make Mum's seventieth birthday a joyful occasion. Mum didn't say a word about Michael in front of my dad or my sister, but whenever we were alone, she would quietly ask me, "Is there any news from Australia?" Every day, my answer remained the same: "Sorry, Mum, not yet." I listened to her pain, quickly understanding that I was really the only person she could confide in. My sister didn't want to hear about it and would quickly shut her down if Michael's name came up. As for my dad, he was a tough and stoic Scotsman who struggled with expressing and handling others' emotions, despite his desire to be supportive.

Six weeks had passed since I sent the email to his adoptive family in Australia, and still there was no response. We found ourselves in a state of helplessness, with nothing more we could do but wait and hope, once again.

Gloria couldn't even tell people "my son has died" because so few people even knew she had a son. She wrote and told Pauline, but they now lived many miles from one another and didn't see one another that often, so once again, when Mum wasn't with me, she found herself grieving alone, trapped in a prison of silence for the second time in her life. The pain and depths of despair for her I know were unbearable, and led to her at times contemplating ending her own life in a desperate desire to end her pain. It was only her love for Bill, for Marie and me and for Georgia that kept her going, and she was selfless in ensuring that she didn't transfer her pain and her grief onto us.

I was not only consumed by intense grief but also by an overwhelming sense of guilt. It was me who had pushed the search forward, me who had posted the advert on the Oz Reunion website, and me who had put pressure on Mum to sign the adoption papers. All I had wanted was to meet my brother and to bring joy and peace to Gloria, yet now I watched her descend into the depths of despair, unable to provide any comfort. As she sank, I sank with her. It was a bleak and helpless period for both of us. She bore the guilt of forty-two years past, and I bore the weight of the present.

'Gloria's 70th Birthday'

CHAPTER 8

Getting to know Mark

Mum and I patiently anticipated a response from Mark's adoptive family in Australia, but alas, day after day, nothing arrived. We wholeheartedly understood and respected their emotions and feelings. They too had suffered the devastating loss of a beloved son and brother, when suddenly, five years after his death, we the long-lost family appeared on their radar. It's only natural that they might have harboured some suspicion about our intentions – what did we want? And why did we choose this moment to try to make contact?

The answer to this was quite straightforward: Gloria was simply and understandably consumed by the need to discover who and what her son had grown up to become. Witnessing her struggling with her grief was heart-wrenching. My father Bill, despite possessing the largest and most compassionate heart, continued to cope with the situation by avoiding discussions and burying his head in the sand, whilst my sister Marie in complete contrast to myself continued to show complete disinterest in the entire matter. Whenever Mum attempted to broach the subject with her, she would vehemently shut her down, openly expressing her unwillingness to engage. This, of course, hurt Mum very deeply.

Each time I spoke with her on the phone or paid her a visit, I was met with an outpouring of "Michael, Michael, Michael ... " " I'm not going to sugar-coat it, at times it became an emotionally draining experience. However, I recognised that I was her sole source of solace in her journey of grief, and as a result I always allowed her to talk, cry, vent, and express her pain, sorrow, and frustration in any way she needed or wanted. Fortunately, I was blessed to have very supportive friends back home who were always on hand to lend an ear when I too required a similar outlet for my feelings.

After discovering that Michael's name had been altered to Mark, I very easily adapted to referring to him as such, and Mark is the name which I shall now continue to use for the rest this story. For Gloria however, he would always remain Michael. That was the name she had lovingly bestowed upon him at birth, and for her it would be forever unchanged.

It was approximately five weeks after we had received the devastating news of Mark's death that I finally received a copy of the adoption papers from Network Seven TV in Sydney. This actually marked the first time I became privy to his adoptive surname. It was then that I began another intense online search, this time diving into Google in pursuit of any information I could find relating his full adoptive name; 'Mark Christopher Stockbridge'* (*Note: Surname changed to protect the identity of his adoptive family).

It's important to recall that I had initially been informed that my brother's death had occurred in 2003, a period when the internet was still very much in its infancy compared to the vast digital landscape we now navigate. Hence, this was a time before the emergence of any of the major social media platforms, so it appeared that Mark had left no digital footprint whatsoever.

All I possessed were the details of the year of his death and the knowledge that it had occurred in the United States. It was a scant amount of information to try to navigate with. Over the course of another six weeks, I tirelessly combed the internet, conducting searches for obituary notices in both the USA and Australia. After much persistence, I stumbled upon a modest obituary notice provided by Smith & Witter Funeral Home in San Francisco: Mark Christopher Stockbridge, born on December 9 1964 – died November 2002. The obituary notice also mentioned his role as a teacher at a Catholic school in Oakland.

Whilst the name and date of birth were indeed a match, the recorded date of death was slightly different to what I'd been told. It was noted here as 2002, whereas the researcher had informed me that he had passed away in 2003. Despite this discrepancy, I felt a strong conviction that it had to be him. With a sense of urgency, I immediately sent an email to the funeral home, providing a brief overview of the situation and requesting any further details they had. I asked whether it was recorded how and where he died? Whether he had been buried or cremated, and other relevant information? Remarkably, I received a response from the funeral home within just a few hours, however they explained that due to the fact his passing had been more than five years earlier, they would require some time to retrieve his file.

True to their word, they called back me just two days later. I had the pleasure of speaking with a very understanding lady who confirmed that they had indeed overseen the arrangements for Mark's funeral. He had been given a direct cremation, and his death certificate indicated AIDS as the cause of his death. What's more, she mentioned that they retained contact information for a man named Clint, who was listed as Mark's executor. She generously provided me with Clint's telephone number and the email address which they held on file from the time of Mark's death.

Given that over five and a half years had passed, I was uncertain whether these contact details would even still be valid. Additionally, I remained in the dark about Clint's role in Mark's life; was he his partner, a friend, or possibly even his attorney? With these uncertainties in mind, I meticulously crafted a lengthy and comprehensive email, taking care to word my message diligently, fully aware that my unsolicited communication could arouse both suspicion and distress.

After another couple of weeks of waiting for a response, I found that anxiety was dragging me down deeper. Uncertainty clouded my mind. I didn't know whether the email address I had been given for Clint was even valid after five years, and hence had no idea whether he had received my message. I decided, slightly apprehensively, to take the plunge and try to call him instead. Clint swiftly answered the phone and confirmed that he had received my email. However, he expressed the need to reach out to Mark's family in Australia, (unaware at the time of my own attempts to contact them) to inform them of my existence before composing a reply; he explained that he too was still awaiting a response from them.

That phone call marked the beginning of a pivotal turning point. Clint immediately proved to be the nicest, sweetest, and most engaging person I could have ever hoped to speak with. His warm Tennessee accent adding to his charm, making me feel like I could listen to him for hours.

During our conversation, Clint reaffirmed that despite the conflicting information regarding the year of Mark's death, this was undoubtedly my brother. He shared with me that Mark had relocated to San Francisco from Sydney around twelve years before he died. Mark had been aware of his adoption for as long as he could remember and had tirelessly searched for his birth mother, especially when he realised that his time here on earth would be limited.

He was desperate to seek his own truth before time ran out. At one point, he had even travelled to England in pursuit of this search, believing that his birth mother had lived in London at the time she became pregnant with him. This was of course based on what the nuns had informed his adoptive parents.

Clint shared that he and Mark were not partners but the closest of friends, alongside another Mark, henceforth referred to as 'Mark 2'. The three of them had forged a deep bond several years earlier and very much considered themselves 'brothers'. As gay men each originating from communities which were not entirely accepting, they had all found themselves seeking the solace of San Francisco, the vibrant epicentre of the LGBTQ community in the United States. Their love and support for each other radiated abundantly from the very first moments of our conversation.

Clint further elaborated on Mark's impressive teaching career.

He told me Mark had been a much loved and exceptionally gifted middle-school teacher at a private Catholic school in San Francisco. His dedication and skill even led him to assume the role of acting principal at one point. Mark's trajectory in teaching seemed exceptionally promising, but as his illness progressed in its later stages, he was regrettably forced to step away from the profession. It was an immense loss not only for Mark himself but also for his colleagues, students, and their families alike.

Mark received the devastating diagnosis of being HIV positive at a tender age of twenty-eight and died nine years later when he was just thirty-seven. Clint assured me that Mark had received exemplary medical care in the USA, being under the supervision of the foremost specialists in HIV and AIDS-related illnesses. He had also explored many alternative therapies in search of relief. Clint fondly reminisced about their shared journey, reflecting, "We laughed together, we cried together, we prayed together, we meditated together ... and we smoked weed together!" Their bond and shared experiences were a mix of laughter, tears, spiritual connections, and moments of solace.

Clint also revealed that Mark possessed a wonderful singing talent, actively participating in a gospel choir at the Glide Ensemble Church in San Francisco. Moreover he was also one of the founding members of the East Oakland Gay Men's Chorus, situated just across the bay. Given my own involvement in numerous choirs over the years, I instantly felt a deep connection with Mark's passion for music. Beyond music, Mark shared a great thirst for travel, just like me, and more notably he thrived on adventure around the globe, just like his birth mother, Gloria. I knew from speaking with Clint that day how effortlessly Mark and Mum would have connected, and it warmed my heart, yet at the same time made it ache with sorrow, knowing this reunion would never be.

Clint and I chatted for what felt like an eternity, and during that time I shed tears of both sadness and joy. It was as if the pieces of a long-awaited puzzle were slowly falling into place. I'm not sure to this day if Clint truly understands just how profoundly significant that conversation was for me and how much I cherish and appreciate him bringing my brother to life through his words. For the first time, Mark evolved from being a mere name and an unknown entity to becoming a tangible person, with a career, hobbies, friends and a compelling story of his own.

As our conversation drew to a close, Clint left me with these poignant words: "Your Australian brother may have passed, but you now have two American brothers in myself and Mark 2." Little did I know then how profoundly true those words would become.

A few days later to my surprise and delight, I received an emotional and heartfelt email from Mark 2. This once again reduced me to tears, and made me laugh out loud as he shared stories from my brother's life, the strength of their friendship and many shared escapades.

Having now gained a wealth of information, I couldn't wait to finally relay it all to Mum. It brought her a huge amount of comfort as I recalled the details from stories which both Clint and Mark 2 had now shared with me. Gloria didn't seem to bat an eyelid with the revelation that her son was gay nor that he had died of AIDS, but in our fairly sheltered world back in England, neither of us had personally known anyone who was HIV positive, nor anyone who had died with AIDS. Mum was generally very open-minded and accepting, but again she had come from this Victorian and Catholic upbringing where being gay was considered a sin, so although she never verbalised it I suspected that inwardly she grappled with the societal expectations of "what would the neighbours say?" She did however speak of her deep sadness caused by the judgement which she now knew both she and her son had been subjected to, and how this 'sinful sex' had not only created Mark's life, but now had also led to the cause of his death. It was a very painful, cruel and unjust fate for both of them.

Mark 2 wasted no time in making copies of the photos he had of Mark, and he sent them across the Atlantic to me. Even though I anticipated their arrival, the moment the envelope landed on my doorstep I could barely contain my excitement. My hands trembled as I picked up the envelope, knowing this was the first time I was going to see my brother's face. Carefully extracting the stack of photos from the envelope, I mindfully glimpsed at the picture on top of the pile. It was a sepia photo of Mark holding one of Mark 2's Chihuahua dogs. I know now that this was one of the later photos taken of Mark, and I could immediately see from that first photo how sick he was. As I looked through all of the photos, a torrent of emotions surged forth just as it had done that very first night I had been informed of his death. I sobbed uncontrollably, I just yearned to embrace him and make it all right, I longed to tell him of the unwavering love that both Gloria and I had held for him for all of these years. I would have given anything to alleviate his suffering – blood, bone marrow, a kidney – I would have quite literally given any part of myself to have saved him.

That night I scanned all the photos, saved them to my computer, and then forwarded them to Mum. For over forty-two years she had clung only to the memory of her baby son's face, and finally, she could behold what a handsome man he had grown up to become. Although Mark had inherited the dark eyes and olive skin from his Italian father, it was also evident that he shared the same nose and mouth as Gloria, and he also bore a close physical resemblance to her father, Percy. The reality of seeing him in photos evoked so many emotions within us both.

Then, just a few days after receiving the photos from America, yet another envelope dropped onto my doormat, this time adorned with Australian postage stamps. I opened it to discover it contained a letter from Mark's adoptive mum.

Michael

CHAPTER 9

Letters from Australia

The letter from Mark's adoptive mother in Australia immediately conveyed heartfelt warmth. It was evident that it came from a lady who was still understandably distraught at losing her son. She explained that only recently, more than five years after the tragic event, had she sought bereavement counselling to help her navigate her deep grief. My unexpected contact had understandably overwhelmed Iris, triggering a resurgence of deep-seated emotions, and her letter highlighted her need to take time to process and navigate through those feelings at her own pace.

Within the letter, Iris recounted the story of how she and her husband, James, came to adopt Mark. She also fondly reminisced about the early days of their life together as a family.

Iris explained that in her twenties she received a diagnosis of an ovarian problem and was given the disheartening prognosis that it was highly unlikely she would ever conceive children naturally. After an unsuccessful and heart-wrenching period of trying to conceive, Iris and James made the decision to try to pursue adoption. Being devout Catholics themselves, the couple reached out to the nuns at the Foundling Home in Waitara, and a short time later they adopted their first daughter Victoria. Lo and behold, however, no sooner had they got Victoria settled into the family home, than to their utter surprise and delight Iris discovered she had fallen pregnant. Nine months later, she gave birth to a beautiful baby boy named Peter. The unexpected turn of events only added an abundance of joy to their family, blending the blessings of adoption and biological parenthood.

The family of four, consisting of Iris, James, Victoria, and Peter, basked in exceptional happiness. Unfortunately, Iris fell ill again shortly after Peter's birth and underwent major surgery. The procedure left her with only a small portion of an ovary, roughly the size of a little fingernail. Peter's conception had already defied all the odds and now the prospect of Iris ever conceiving again seemed to depend on nothing short of a miracle.

Iris and James had always harboured the desire for a larger family though, so for a second time they contacted the nuns at Waitara and enquired about the possibility of adopting another child. The nuns swiftly responded, inviting them for a meeting.

During this meeting the nuns revealed, "we have a little baby boy upstairs if you'd like to meet him. His birth mother would really love for him to be raised within the Catholic faith." Iris and James eagerly accepted the invitation and were immediately taken up to meet the newborn named 'Michael'. Cuddling him in their arms, they instantly fell head over heels in love with him. Then, in next to no time, adoption was legally finalised. Iris joyfully recounted, "we brought him home early in the New Year."

The New Year? Wait – when Gloria left her baby at ten days old, around 19th December, she was told that he was going home to his adoptive family that very day. She was always comforted by the belief that her baby was in the arms of his new family in time for Christmas. (I later went on to meet Iris in person – more about that in another chapter – but she further confirmed that yes, they definitely brought baby Michael home in the New Year.) When the nuns took baby Michael from Gloria's arms, assuring her that he was going home with his adoptive family that very day, it was a fabricated scenario. In reality, Michael spent his first Christmas alone in the nursery at the mother and baby home, and Gloria had absolutely no idea. She had entrusted her baby to the nuns that day, all washed, dressed, and wrapped up ready to be placed in the care of his new mummy and daddy.

Despite my urge to share this painful truth with Gloria, I never did. It would change nothing now. This disclosure would quite simply shatter the pieces of her already broken heart. As time passed though, it became evident that this was just one of many falsehoods conveyed by the nuns, to both Gloria and to the adoptive parents Iris and James. A web of deception woven by the nuns was now unfolding, and I wondered in reality how many other lives were affected by similar means after adoption through the mother and baby home in Waitara.

As mentioned earlier, after his adoption baby Michael was lovingly renamed Mark. Mark seamlessly integrated into his new family and was warmly welcomed as the youngest of three children. Victoria and Peter adored their new baby brother. Mark had been with the family just a few short months though when another miracle occurred, Iris discovered to her complete disbelief and great joy that she was pregnant once again, and hence another nine months later Mark became a 'big brother' to Nicholas. Now if two miracles were not already enough, Iris very quickly fell pregnant again and the family was completed with the arrival of a baby girl named Melissa. Mark now stood as the third of five children, and Iris and James found themselves with their hands quite full, navigating the challenges of raising five children in a span of just about as many years. The household was bustling with the joy and energy that come with a growing brood. Together, they forged an extraordinarily happy and close-knit family, and Mark's formative years unfolded in the scenic embrace of the Blue Mountains, nestled on the outskirts of Sydney.

Then, out of the blue, tragedy struck unexpectedly when Mark was just six years old. His father James died suddenly from a heart attack at the tender age of just thirty-eight. This devastating event not only left Iris widowed, but also thrust upon her the daunting responsibility of single-handedly raising her five grieving children.

In the aftermath of James's passing, the family had to make adjustments, downsizing their home and relocating from the Blue Mountains to a residence in the Beverly Hills area of Sydney. This new setting would become Iris's home for many years to come. Iris never remarried, and she devoted herself entirely to raising her children, and to the Catholic Church, within which she found both solace and support. She fully embraced the role of a dedicated mother, and as the years passed she evolved into a cherished and much-loved grandmother to numerous grandchildren, as all four of her other children went on to have families of their own.

Iris's deep and profound grief over losing Mark was palpable, and her love for him shone through in her writing. As she recounted her story, it was evident that she never made any distinction between her 'biological' children and her 'adopted' children. To her, they were all simply her children and that was the unequivocal truth.

When I wrote back to Iris, I provided her with Gloria's address, and for a while the two of them engaged in a heart-warming exchange of handwritten letters. This was immensely healing and cathartic for both mothers. In parallel, Gloria also began a regular exchange of emails with Mark 2 in California, and bit by bit the pieces of Mark's life, with all of its highs and lows, started to come together.

In one of her letters to Gloria, Iris told her that Mark had been aware of his adoption from a very young age. She assured Gloria that she had presented him with the christening gown and Bible that had been given to him as a baby, and he had known it was a gift filled with love from his birth mother. Iris had also known for many years that Mark had a deep desire to find his birth mother and had offered him her unwavering support, as she had done with everything else throughout his life.

In contrast, apparently Mark's older adopted sister Victoria had never expressed any interest in tracing her birth family, showing that people's individual journey and curiosity about their origins can vary significantly.

It continued to remain a mystery, however, how with Gloria and Mark both on the same adoption reunion register in Australia for so many years, they had not been able to find one another? It was to be almost another three years when I was on the other side of the world that the answer to this mystery would finally reveal itself.

Before any trip was ever planned to Australia though, a trip was to be made to San Francisco. I was in regular communication with both Clint and Mark 2, who were, without even a meeting in person, quickly becoming like brothers to me. I cherished them deeply, a sentiment that remains true to this day.

In the spring of 2010, two years after we had received the heart-breaking news of Mark's death, I boarded a plane to San Francisco, accompanied by my daughter Georgia, who then was twelve years old. Unfortunately, Gloria was suffering with some health problems at the time which prevented her from joining us on this long journey. Nevertheless, I committed to living these experiences on her behalf, diligently sharing with her every story, photo, and memory of her son along the way. Little did I know as we embarked the plane, that this journey would surpass all of our expectations.

Mark 2 (left), 'our' Mark (centre), Clint (right). Circa 2000.

CHAPTER 10

Your Love Echoes around the World

Reflecting on the emotional maturity exhibited by my daughter Georgia at the age of just twelve makes me incredibly proud. She became my pillar of strength, my steadfast companion, and my constant source of support during a very turbulent time in our lives.

The prospect of spending two weeks in San Francisco lay before us, and I found myself carrying a complete mix of emotions; excitement, nervousness and of course a huge amount of sentimentality. Clint, along with his partner Jeff, was already living in the Bay Area at the time, and Mark 2 was embarking on a ten-hour drive up from his hometown in Palm Springs. I think we all were experiencing both a sense of excitement and emotional anticipation.

From the first time Georgia and I met these three beautiful men any worries or fears I had been harbouring just melted away. We had already been communicating for around two years and forged a strong foundation, but meeting in person compounded this instant loving connection and over the next couple of weeks our connections blossomed. We laughed, we cried, we listened and we talked. Summing up the depth of that experience in just one chapter is a daunting task; I could easily fill a whole book based solely on the richness of our interactions during that time. What I can say however, is that the impact of that trip resonated on such a deep and intense level that words can only capture a fraction of its depth.

For me this trip was somewhat of a pilgrimage, a journey of discovery, partly for myself and very much so for Gloria. However, for Clint and Mark 2 they had lost their brother seven and a half years earlier and grieved hard for him. Having navigated that dark tunnel of sorrow, both before and after Mark's death, and emerged through the other end into a brighter existence, they were now walking in Mark's footsteps once again, returning to the many places they had been together, sharing stories of both his living and his dying, confronting triggers, and revisiting both joyful and painful memories. They willingly plunged themselves back into that tunnel of grief. They didn't have to do this, yet they walked that path for us – to show us Mark, to share with us his life, his loves, his achievements, and his fears. To this day, I'm uncertain whether they fully comprehend the immense gratitude we owe them. The love we experienced during that time is unparalleled, and will forever remain an extraordinary presence in my life.

It is said that you can tell a lot about a man by the company he keeps, and on meeting Mark 2 and Clint and swiftly discovering how vibrant, loving, generous and fun they were, it became evident that this was a direct reflection of the person that Mark was. His personality mirrored the friends he had attracted into his life, and the love that he was surrounded in to the very last day of that life. Although Jeff hadn't known Mark personally, having met and formed a relationship with Clint after Mark's passing, he played a substantial role in the enchanting and magical time we shared during those weeks in the Bay. His presence added to the richness of our collective experience, creating lasting memories of a time sealed by love and connection.

Our Mark had spent the last twelve years of his life living in San Francisco, a city which he loved, and a place where he felt a sense of belonging. Diagnosed as HIV positive at the age of twenty-eight, he fought the virus with everything he had until he died just ten days before his thirty-eighth birthday. I have been given the honour of reading from Mark's personal diaries covering some of those years, including his reflection on his moment of diagnosis. Out of respect for the deeply personal nature of those memoirs am not going to divulge much here. However I can share that his writings contained a raw reflection of fear, shame, stigma, bewilderment, and the loss of a very bright future which should have lain ahead for him. These intimate entries offer a window into the complex emotions Mark grappled with as he navigated the challenges of living with HIV.

Mark was a victim of the devastating AIDS pandemic which swept through the heart of the gay community in San Francisco from the late 1980s. This epidemic claimed the lives of thousands, and for people such as Mark 2 and Clint they didn't just lose one friend or brother, they each lost dozens.

I wasn't familiar with that world and I admit that HIV/AIDS hadn't even been on my radar for most of my life, nor for those within my social circles. It is only subsequently as I have become a part of my brother's community that I have gained a deeper understanding of the extensive loss, fear and grief which engulfed not only the gay community of San Francisco but so many others worldwide.

While exploring San Francisco during our visit, we immersed ourselves in the iconic sights such as the Golden Gate Bridge, Alcatraz, and the charming street cars. However, a significant portion of our time was dedicated to what we fondly referred to as "Mark-seeing." The boys guided us through numerous locations that held special significance for Mark – places he lived and cherished. We strolled through his favourite park adorned with Japanese botanical gardens, dined at the restaurants he loved, and visited the schools where he passionately taught. The journey also took us to the apartments both in San Francisco and across the Bay in Oakland, providing poignant glimpses into the various chapters of his life – the places where he laughed, loved, and ultimately, where he passed away.

The boys shared with me that they had lost contact with Mark's former partner, Alonzo, with whom he had spent many significant years, even though they were not together at the time of Mark's passing. Despite the separation, they believed Alonzo was still residing in the Bay Area. Intrigued, I located Alonzo on Facebook and reached out to him. To my delight he replied almost instantaneously and extended a warm invitation for us to visit him in his home the very next day, signing off his message "Mi casa es su casa" translated to "my house is your house". During our visit he generously painted vivid pictures of the life they once shared, which included their first date, their first kiss, and their most loving moments, right down to Mark's hissy fits when he wasn't happy with something!

In a touching revelation, Alonzo shared with us a treasure trove of handwritten love letters he had kept, which Mark had sent him during his visits back to Australia to spend time with his family. To see my brother's handwriting and read his heartfelt words was both powerful and deeply moving; it somehow brought him to life much more than photos had and made him very much more tangible. Over those two weeks I truly felt I got know Mark and finally had a relationship with my brother, as I had a vivid picture of him which transcended the limitation of imagination. Maybe not the relationship I had dreamed of having for all those years but nevertheless a heartfelt connection which brought him to life, in a way which photographs never quite could.

Gloria obviously took huge comfort from this too. Despite her physical absence during the trip, she remained an integral part of our journey. I consistently kept her updated through texts and emails, recounting every intricate detail and story while they were still vivid in my mind. I remained painfully aware that every step I took during this extraordinary pilgrimage was a link between Gloria and her beloved son.

Despite Alonzo and Mark having ended their romantic relationship sometime before Mark's death, they maintained a remarkably close friendship. Even seven years after Mark's passing, Alonzo still held a deep affection for him. Alonzo fondly recalled an annual tradition on Mark's birthday when he would always buy him a dozen red roses, and how they would share a slow dance in the kitchen to their favourite song. In the years following Mark's death, Alonzo continued this ritual by visiting Mark's old apartment and leaving a red rose on the doorstep, before returning home, playing their song, and engaging in a symbolic slow dance with Mark's memory in the kitchen. To know Mark had known such love, and to know that this love still continued beyond the grave, was phenomenally beautiful.

Alonzo was also HIV positive but by the time we met also had oral cancer and already knew his illness was now terminal as the cancer had spread to his lungs. He had been given anything between one and seven years to live. Reflecting on his own mortality he told me, "Mark taught me how to live well, and he also taught me how to die well. When my time comes I hope I can be as brave and as dignified as he was and to experience death in the same beautiful way."

During my time with Alonzo, I found it challenging to fully understand his speech. He explained that just a few months prior, he had undergone surgery to remove half of his tongue. Alonzo had been diagnosed as HIV positive many years before, pre-dating his meeting with Mark (although Mark did not contract it this way), which now left his immune system compromised.

Mark had passed away just a few days after American Thanksgiving in 2002, a time he previously cherished, having written in his diary just the year a year earlier that this was his favourite part of the year. He had a deep appreciation for the gathering of friends and family, free from the materialistic aspects so often associated with Christmas.

During Mark's final hours, even when he was no longer conscious, his friends gathered by his bedside to continue the celebration of Thanksgiving with him. They sang, spoke to him, and offered prayers. When he passed away in his Oakland apartment on November 29th 2002, he was enveloped in the love of his friends and family from both the USA and Australia. Iris, Peter, and Melissa had all flown over to be with him, providing a comforting and reassuring presence during his transition.

When I returned home from San Francisco I continued to keep in touch and correspond via email with Alonzo, but almost exactly a year later I saw tributes flooding onto his Facebook page and realised with the deepest sorrow that he too had died. I take comfort that in a better world beyond our sight Mark and Alonzo still slow dance together among the stars.

During our initial visit to Clint and Jeff's apartment, Clint pointed out an urn which sat in his living room. He gently said "that's your brother" as he handed it to me to hold. After years of yearning to hug and hold my brother, he was now in my arms, represented by nothing more than cremated ashes in an urn. Yet, the overwhelming rush of love I felt in that physical connection has stayed with me to this day. Clint went on to explain that, as per Mark's own request, half of his cremains had been sent back to Australia for his family there, while the other half stayed with Clint in America. Totally unexpectedly, Clint then said, "Now it's time to return him to his birth family. I know this is what he would want." I was rendered speechless; this was the very last thing I had anticipated, yet its significance was immeasurable. More importantly, I knew exactly how much this was going to mean to Gloria as well.

Another of the most profound moments of our visit occurred on Easter Sunday morning when Clint and Mark 2 took us to the Glide Memorial Church – this is a church the likes of which I have never experienced in my life, they don't have services, they have 'celebrations' and welcome people of every diversity and orientation. Notably, public figures such as Hillary Clinton have been known to attend, alongside drug addicts, homeless people, the LGBTQ+ community, and all people for whom none of us really need labels. It was an incredibly accepting and non-judgemental experience, a rarity that could make the world a much better place if there were more like it. This is the church where Mark used to sing in the gospel choir, the place where he found 'his tribe' and where his friends became his family. Their celebration includes a time where people are invited to stand up and openly share their stories. In turn Clint courageously stood up and said, "many of you will remember your friend and choir member Mark S…….." He went on to share the quest of Mark's search for his birth family, which had continued until his time ran out, and shared that five years after Mark's passing he himself had received a telephone call from a lady in England who was Mark's biological sister, and now she, and her daughter, Mark's niece, were present at the Glide sitting right next to him!

Cheers and applause went out from the choir and from the entire congregation. To this day I am in awe of Clint's inner strength in standing up and telling that story, because I, Georgia and Mark 2 all sat there sobbing like babies.

My sole disappointment during the trip was discovering that the next concert of the East Oakland Gay Men's Chorus, of which Mark had been a founder member, was scheduled a week after our departure. I would have cherished the opportunity to witness their performance, but perhaps that was going to be a reason for a return visit in the future.

Our two weeks in San Francisco passed by in a flash, seeming far too short. It had been a whirlwind of emotions, yet a time filled with beauty, friendship, love, and joy. Memories which I determined would prevail over the undercurrent of loss and grief. Perhaps I was inspired by a quote from Mark's own diary, again written about year before his death, where he had said, "I am also thankful for HIV/AIDS because it has brought angels into my life, angels I would not have otherwise met." I endeavoured to live by his words. Due to his passing, these angels, Clint, Mark 2, Jeff, and Alonzo, had entered my and Georgia's life, sharing something with us (and, in turn, Gloria) that I can never fully capture in writing this story.

All too soon, it was time to bid some tearful goodbyes. Mark 2 was leaving the Bay to drive home to Palm Springs, and we were scheduled to fly out the next day to return to England. With a heavy heart, I logged on online to check in for our flights, but check-in was denied. Cutting another long story short, we quickly discovered that the Eyjafjallajökul volcano had erupted in Iceland, sending a plume of volcanic ash more than 9km into the sky and forcing UK airspace to close.

After an entire night of unsuccessful attempts to contact the airline over the phone, we decided to make a trip to San Francisco airport to try to gain some insight into exactly what was happening. After queuing for over three hours, we were informed that the earliest flight we could secure to get home would be two weeks later. Were we sorry about this? Not a chance! The smile on Georgia's face grew wider and wider as she realised she would be missing the first two weeks of the new school term. Moreover, the prospect of spending an extra two weeks in San Francisco, in a new hotel, all expenses covered by British Airways along with $100 food vouchers per day, was music to our ears.

As we returned to downtown San Francisco, Clint came to meet us so we could move our luggage to the new hotel. He laughed and said, "This was all your brother's work, you know, now you can go to the Oakland Gay Men's Chorus concert next weekend. It was meant to be!"

And so it was that we enjoyed another glorious two weeks in California, some of it still in San Francisco with Clint and Jeff, and a few days down in San Jose staying with some family friends whom we hadn't had time to see in our first two weeks. Of course the highlight of our extended visit was the fact that we got to see the Oakland Gay Men's Chorus in concert, and meet some more of Mark's old friends. It was yet another experience which I shall never ever forget. As they ended their performance with a spine tingling rendition of 'What a Wonderful World', tears rolled down my cheeks. Clint put his arm around me and hugged me tightly. It truly is a wonderful world and I knew in that moment that Mark wanted me to see it all, he wanted me to continue the adventures which both Gloria and he had started. The love of travel most certainly ran through our DNA.

When the time finally came for us to return home, I packed up my most precious cargo, Mark's ashes, and carried them close to me in my hand luggage along with additional documentation provided to me by Clint. We bade our final goodbyes to Clint and Jeff at the airport and proceeded through security. As we presented our tickets for the final inspection at the boarding gate, the machine beeped, and the staff member said, "Wait one minute, please." The worst scenarios ran through my mind, given the confusion with our earlier cancelled flights, and I assumed there was going to be an additional problem. However, in less than a minute, the airport assistant added, "You've both got a free upgrade to business class!" It was the first time in my life that I had ever flown business class, and both Georgia and I were beaming from ear to ear. "That was Mark," I said to Georgia, "he didn't want to fly home in economy."

On return home I had a beautiful new urn crafted for Mark's ashes; on the lid was a sunflower (which I had learnt was his favourite flower) and the sides were adorned with an exquisite image of the Golden Gate Bridge and a panoramic view of San Francisco. On Mum's next visit to us, I handed her the box. "I can finally hold my baby in my arms again," she whispered with tears in her eyes. I couldn't even find the words to respond, I just nodded silently, then slipped out of the room to give her some privacy. Gloria was finally reunited with her son, but not in a way that either of us had ever visualised.

Gloria loved the San Francisco urn though and she said, "can you have one made for me when I die please, only I want Sydney Harbour on mine because that's where a piece of my heart will always be." I promised her that when the time came I would make it happen.

CHAPTER 11

The Gown

There was another significant narrative which came out of meeting Mark 2, a story to which Gloria felt so deeply connected that I deemed it deserving of its own dedicated chapter.

The initial meeting between Mark and Mark 2, (later affectionately known as Mark squared) unfolded in the spring of 1994. Their paths converged at the Glide Memorial Church in San Francisco where, as previously mentioned, Mark was a member of the Glide Ensemble, the church's resident gospel choir. This particular evening held extraordinary significance as the choir was in the process of recording a live CD in front of the congregation. Adding to the momentous occasion, the late and esteemed Maya Angelou was scheduled to grace the stage alongside them.

On that memorable evening, Mark assumed his place in the choir whilst Mark 2 was ushering in the congregation. Their first meeting was the start of a beautiful friendship, and before long they found themselves sharing an apartment as housemates.

During those early days of house sharing, their closeness was a far cry from what it would evolve into in subsequent years. They approached their initial living arrangement with a degree of caution, tiptoeing around each other and respecting the need for space and privacy that each one required.

On this particular day Mark 2 returned home from work and as he entered the apartment, he had to pass by Mark's bedroom door. As he passed by, he noticed that the door was slightly ajar, and he could hear the sound of crying emanating from within. Respecting the boundaries that existed between them, he hesitated to intrude immediately. However, after a few minutes concern outweighed restraint, prompting him to revisit Mark's room to ensure everything was OK. Through the gap in the slightly opened door he could see Mark sitting on the bed holding something close to him.

Mark 2 gently knocked and slowly opened the bedroom door; upon entering he said he could see Mark holding a small white gown, and next to him on the bed was a parcel marked from Sydney. Mark 2 obviously had no idea what it was, nor the connection, so with genuine concern he put his arm around Mark and enquired, "what do you have?" Mark could not answer, completely overwhelmed he simply broke down in tears. Mark 2, understanding nothing other than the depth of Mark's emotion, embraced him and allowed him to release this huge tsunami of feeling.

As Mark's tears gradually subsided, he began to share the significance of this parcel with Mark 2. Iris had sent it to him unexpectedly from Australia, along with a letter explaining that this was his christening gown which had been gifted to him with love by his birth mother at the time of his adoption. As Mark 2 recounted this poignant tale to me many years later, he too could barely get the words out. I could tell that as he recalled these memories he was transported back into that room, and he was there once again, embracing Mark in this highly emotional moment they had shared. Mark 2 said, "that afternoon he was the closest to Gloria that he had ever been, he felt her. It was both a moment of elation and devastation for him."

Even as I type this now, two decades after Mark's death, I do so with tears streaming down my face. Mark 2 portrayed the imagery of this moment with such tenderness and beauty, capturing every ounce of the intense emotion. The irony is so cruel; Gloria desperately longed to find her son, whilst Mark desperately wanted to find his birth mum. A tiny white christening gown was the only conduit connecting the deep love they held for one another and their desire to be reunited.

Curious about the gown's current whereabouts, I enquired of Mark 2, "Where is the christening gown now?" He responded with some uncertainty, saying, "I'm really not sure, I can only assume that Iris took it back with her to Australia after Mark passed."

A fragment of my heart had always been in Australia too, yet at the age of forty I had still never set foot there. It became clear that this needed to be the next step in our personal journey. So, ten months after our visit to San Francisco, Georgia and I once again boarded a plane. This time our destination was Down Under, as we embarked on a journey to meet Mark's adoptive family. Sadly, once again Gloria's own health prohibited her from making such a long journey.

CHAPTER 12

Australia, Meetings, Lies and New Life

In February 2011, I found myself with the need to visit Melbourne, driven by both personal and professional reasons. The International College of Celebrancy, with whom I then collaborated on my celebrancy training business, had their base in Melbourne. The forthcoming chapter will shed light on the additional personal reasons that prompted this visit.

Knowing I would be visiting Melbourne anyway, it felt crazy to be in Australia and not seize the opportunity to take a flight across to Sydney to meet with Mark's adoptive family. Iris by now had engaged in a large amount of correspondence with both Gloria and me. While the relationship was not as open, welcome, and loving as the one with the boys in the USA, we were all steadily building a comfortable rapport. Most importantly, Gloria was gaining insights into her son's early years in Australia, and I believe Iris found comfort in being able to share stories of her son, and find someone who would have a deeper empathy, given their shared grief.

In a leap of faith, I chose to pen another letter to Iris. I explained that Georgia and I were planning to be in Melbourne and wondered how she would feel regarding a face-to-face meeting if we were to fly up to Sydney for a day or two. I desperately wanted to meet her, more so for Gloria's sake than for my own; to witness her in person, to see her face, feel her energy, hear her voice, and see the house where

Mark had spent a significant part of his younger life. I didn't want to push things though, so I tried to approach the situation delicately. I knew Iris was still grieving badly for Mark and I did not want to impose anything on her which made her feel under pressure or might deepen her grief in any way.

An email quickly arrived in response, via Iris's youngest son Nicholas, not only expressing agreement to meet with us but also extending an invitation for a two-day stay in her home. This unexpected and generous gesture overwhelmed me, as it was far more than I had anticipated. Nevertheless I accepted the invitation immediately, filled with immense gratitude.

Georgia and I made travel arrangements to fly to Melbourne first, then fly across to Sydney for a two-day visit before returning to Melbourne. This marked my inaugural trip to Australia, and I very deliberately chose not to fly directly into Sydney first. For so many years, I had dreamed of and visualised landing there to reunite with my brother in the arrivals hall. Knowing now that this would never be a reality, I opted for a domestic flight rather than an international one. Somehow this seemed to soften the emotional impact, albeit just a little.

On arrival into Melbourne we were met around midnight by Dally Messenger who is the principal of the International College of Celebrancy in Australia and who was the primary reason for my business trip there.

Following a wonderful week in Melbourne we flew on to Sydney. As I walked into that arrivals hall, my eyes welled up with tears. It was harder than I had expected, or tried to mentally prepare myself for. There was no one there to meet us as Georgia and I had planned to get the train from Sydney Airport out to Beverly Hills which was the area of Sydney where Iris lived.

It was just a short walk from the station to Iris's house and as soon as we met her any lingering nerves instantly melted away. To our surprise, not only was Iris there to welcome us, but all of Mark's siblings (except his eldest sister, Victoria) along with their spouses and children. It turned out to be a grand family gathering and one into which we were warmly welcomed with open arms.

We enjoyed a delightful lunch and a wonderful afternoon getting to know these friendly and welcoming people. However, there was one noticeable absence – Mark!

His name remained unspoken, a silent agreement among all, as if a collective fear lingered, preventing anyone from being the first to utter it. Everyone, including myself, seemed apprehensive about upsetting the delicate balance in the company. I was feeling increasingly uncomfortable with this elephant in the room. I so longed to hear all of their stories and memories but naturally didn't want to push this on anyone.

It wasn't until much later that evening when the siblings and their families had departed to their respective homes, and we were alone with Iris, that she finally opened up and started to talk about Mark. There was still much information to exchange; we wanted to know about Mark's story and she wanted to know about Gloria's story. It was in this revealing conversation that the depth of the nuns' deception started to become evident. Firstly, Iris confirmed that whilst Mark's adoption had been agreed in December 1964, she and James did not bring him home until after the New Year, meaning that whilst Gloria had been sent away from Waitara believing that her baby son would be with his new family for Christmas, but this was most definitely not the case. Iris, on the other hand, spent Christmas believing that the baby's birth mother was still caring for him, Yet for reasons unknown this poor innocent tiny baby, who was already loved and cherished by two mothers, spent his first Christmas without either and in the sole care of the nuns at Waitara Foundling Home.

Furthermore, Iris had been informed that Mark's birth mother was an English nurse who fallen pregnant in England, was transported to Australia to give birth, and was then promptly sent back home. Except for the detail of Gloria being an English nurse, none of the rest of the information which the nuns had given them was accurate. When Iris discovered the truth, tears welled up in her eyes as she expressed, "If we had known for one moment that Gloria had remained here alone in Australia, we would have helped her and had contact with her. We would never have allowed her to be abandoned in the way that she was."

Perhaps though, the most significant deception of all came to light when Iris revealed why Gloria and Mark had never been reunited on the register. At the time of the adoption, the paperwork provided to Iris and her husband indicated that the baby's birth mother was named Ann, not Gloria. Unlike today's adoptions involving social services, this was a completely private arrangement. Shockingly, it appeared that the nuns at Waitara had forged the adoption records, leading to the false identity of Mark's birth mother as Ann instead of her real name.

As my searches over the years for my brother remained fruitless because Gloria did not know her son's adopted name, at the same time Mark traversed the world in search of a mother named Ann. This cruel deliberate deception perpetrated by the Catholic nuns was the crucial element that prevented Mark from ever discovering the depth of love and affection his birth mother held for him. Tragically, Mark passed away without the knowledge of this connection, leaving Gloria to endure the remainder of her life with a shattered heart, never having the chance to reunite with her son before his death.

Our time spent with Iris and her family was both exceptional and cathartic. One of the few honest things which Gloria had been told at the time of her baby's adoption was that she couldn't ask for a nicer family to raise her son, and in meeting Iris I fully believe that to be true.

Iris's love and devotion to her whole family radiated abundantly. In addition, sleeping in the house which was Mark's home since he was six also gave me an incredible sense of connection. Being able to share further photos and stories with Gloria of the house where Mark was raised and of the family that played such an integral role in his upbringing, helped her enormously in her attempts to navigate the depths of her grief. The trauma, guilt and concern she had held within her for so many years having given her baby up to be raised by another family, and the crippling grief and depression she had suffered on learning of his death.

On the second day of our visit, Mark's older brother Peter took me, Georgia, Iris and his own young son to Featherdale Zoo in Sydney. This was about an hour's car journey from their home. I didn't feel at all well in the car on the way there and as the day went on, I felt worse and worse. I wanted to be on top form as we excitedly hand-fed kangaroos and cuddled koalas, but instead I began to feel increasingly nauseous and dizzy as the hours passed. By the time we arrived back at Iris's house, I had to excuse myself from the meal she was preparing and go and lie down in the bedroom.

I had only experienced this overwhelming sense of heady nausea once in my life before, thirteen years earlier when I was pregnant with Georgia. By now my period was already a few days late, and I had attributed it to the strains of travel, stress and emotion. However, as I now lay on the bed in Mark's childhood home, I placed my hand on my tummy and without even doing a test, I instinctively knew that there was a new little life growing inside of me. Gloria was going to have a new grandchild.

CHAPTER 13

History Repeats Itself

Perhaps this is one of the hardest chapters for me to write, given its deeply personal nature. I admit I had a slight internal battle as to whether to include it or not, but it is very much part of the fabric which weaves this whole story together.

In 1997, at the age of twenty-six, I gave birth to my first-born child Georgia. Interestingly, this was the same age at which Gloria gave birth to Michael. I too was a single, unmarried mother from the moment of Georgia's birth. Fortunately, after thirty-three years, societal prejudice against unmarried mothers has undergone a significant and positive transformation, or I too might have found myself in the same position as Gloria. The idea of my newborn daughter being taken away from me was unthinkable.

I had been in a relationship with her biological father for around eleven months when I fell pregnant. The first few months of our relationship had been idyllic, but pretty soon cracks began to emerge. Emotional and psychological abuse quickly evolved into physical abuse. He was a stereotypical narcissist, but at the age of twenty-five/twenty-six I don't think I even comprehended the concept of narcissism. Friends and family had seen through him much sooner than I had. I was young and in love so when things started falling apart, I didn't want to admit the truth to anyone, least of all myself. As I mentioned in a previous chapter, my dad was a hard Scotsman and if he had known the extent of my ordeal I truly believed he would have killed him, and ended up in jail himself! Naturally I was never going to risk that happening and so I stayed quiet and suffered in silence.

The abuse continued and escalated until I reached four and a half months into my pregnancy. It was at this stage that the violence had intensified to such an extent that I knew I had to get out for the safety of my unborn child. I was broken-hearted because I was, perhaps very foolishly and naively, still in love with this monster of a man. Given my own Catholic upbringing and personal pride, I loathed the prospect of being single mother, because even though society had become much more accepting there were still lingering labels and stereotypes attached to the term. I was broken and afraid, afraid of him and afraid of my future as a lone parent. What I did know and value though, was that I had the unwavering love and support of my parents, as well as from many great friends.

The 8th of September 1997 marked the day I became a mother for the first time. It truly was the happiest day of my life to date. In that moment, I realised that I didn't need a man in my life; I had Georgia, and that was all that mattered. I would be both a mother and a father to her, and she would want for nothing. I had never experienced a love or bond so profound and deep. I gave birth with my dear friend Shelley by my side, and with both Gloria and Bill meeting their first grandchild in the middle of the night, when she was less than an hour old.

In those earliest days of motherhood, I gained a much deeper understanding of what my mum must have endured when she had her baby all alone on the other side of the world, and the devastating loss she must have experienced in having to give him up. Now, as a lone parent myself, I was fortunate to have my parents visiting us daily, showering us with love and affection, as well as helping out in numerous practical ways. Although Mum never explicitly expressed it, I sensed that this brought back painful memories for her, and she harboured a sense of longing for what might have been had she given birth to her own son a generation later.

Gloria loved being a nana, she embraced the role and doted on her new granddaughter at every opportunity. Without her help, and of course that of my dad, I honestly don't know where I would have been.

I did meet another man, Chris, just eight weeks after Georgia was born. We met whilst both performing in an amateur dramatics production of Fiddler on the Roof and three years later we got married. Chris proved to be an incredible father to Georgia, never hesitating in bringing her up as his own flesh and blood. He was a lovely man with the biggest caring heart. However, there was an eighteen-year age gap between us (he had in fact played the role of Tevye – my father in Fiddler on the Roof!) and as much as I had wanted and needed a father figure for Georgia, I quickly found myself feeling trapped and very unhappy. I struggled for several years to try to make it work, desperately trying to salvage our family life together, but as time went on we drifted further apart in our marriage and had to admit it was over. Nevertheless, to this day Chris remains one of my best friends, and continues to be a loyal and devoted father to Georgia.

For many years, I often reflected that I had succeeded in almost every aspect of my life ... except relationships, and for a significant part of my life, I was pretty much going it alone as a single parent, albeit Georgia and Chris maintained a strong father-daughter relationship. I dated on and off, and throughout all of my thirties held a deep desire to have another child, I dreamed about it and longed for it with all my heart. Yet, as my fortieth birthday approached, and Georgia turned thirteen, I had to acknowledge to myself that I was destined to have only ever have one child.

In the summer of 2010 I engaged in conversation with a pallbearer at work whilst waiting in a cemetery for a family to say their final goodbyes at the graveside (not the most romantic setting, but hey, I had worked in the funeral profession for many years, there was always going to be a chance of such connections). His Australian accent immediately captivated me. Despite having seen him around on and off for several months, during the times I was working with this particular funeral home, this was the first time we had entered into conversation. Admittedly, it was his accent that initially piqued my interest, though I kept that to myself. He told me during that conversation however that he had a ticket booked back to Australia and would be going home in a couple of weeks' time. We said our goodbyes and I thought nothing more of it.

Later that evening, a friend request from 'Christopher Trickey,' or 'Trickey' as he was familiarly known at work, popped up in my Facebook notifications. Intrigued, I accepted, and soon after a message arrived in my direct mailbox. He told me how much he had liked me for months but never had the courage to strike up conversation until that day. Despite not being one to usually make swift moves, he explained that his imminent return to Australia prompted him to reach out, proposing a meet-up for a drink. Agreeing, we set a date, and during the remaining short time, our connection deepened and I found that I was quickly harbouring strong feelings for him. Then, all too soon, he was gone, back to Melbourne, and I honestly believed that our very brief story had reached its conclusion.

Unexpectedly, Trickey then messaged me from Australia, and we corresponded on social media for the next few months. By the New Year I already knew I needed to try to get out to Australia for work. I obviously desperately wanted to meet Iris as well, so it now seemed as if there was an element of additional fate built in that I would also now be able to see Trickey and decide whether any form of long-term relationship was worth pursuing.

The date was set, and flight tickets were booked for the following month in February. My excitement grew by the day; I was finally going to set foot in Australia for the first time and already had so much to look forward to there, and the thought of seeing Trickey again was the icing on the cake, not that I told him that. As a single mother, it was only natural I would be taking Georgia with me on this journey, and she was almost as excited as I was.

However, my excitement was slightly dampened when I received another message from Trickey. "I applied for my old job back in the UK – they said yes but want me to come back immediately. The good news is that I'll see you sooner, the bad news is I won't be in Melbourne when you visit." Whilst the latter was a little disheartening, I already knew our trip to Australia was going to be phenomenal and we would be making the most of every single day, so I didn't dwell on it for more than a couple of minutes.

So back he came to England, just one week before I left for Australia. It was a passionate and tender reunion, having not seen one another for all those months, and things moved quickly knowing that I would be leaving again in only a week's time.

From the outset I was aware that he had only returned to England on a twelve-month visa and we had had no plans for a long-term relationship. Nevertheless, we had feelings for one another and that was at least good enough to build foundations on.

Fast forward to our time in Sydney, where I was staying in Mark's childhood home. Despite battling severe nausea, I clawed my way back to Melbourne the following day and took the test which confirmed what I already strongly suspected – I was pregnant, and my baby's father was Australian!

I had no idea how Trickey was going to react, and so I grappled with the revelation relating to this unexpected turn of events. I had gone from being in a marriage with a man eighteen years older than me, to the very early stages of a relationship with a man twelve years younger than me. I was forty at this stage and Trickey was twenty-eight.

I honestly didn't know how to tell him. Anything we had between us was still so new, we were not even 'officially' in a relationship, and the only time children had ever come up in conversation, he had strongly verbalised that he didn't want any! I hadn't dwelled on this, as at the age of forty I thought I was past it anyway. However, I knew what whatever the outcome now, I wanted this baby more than anything in the world. I had already done the lone parenting once and I was more than prepared to do it again if I had to.

I sat outside on the steps at the International Square in Melbourne. I took a deep breath and sent him a long text message. It started with, "I know this is a million miles from what we had planned, but…" I went on to pour my heart out to him and immediately gave him options to be in or out as a parent. The reply came back within seconds, the stark and heart-wrenching reply simply read "TERMINATE THAT

CHILD, IT WON'T HAVE A FATHER".

My heart sank at Trickey's response. While I had half-expected him to express hesitations about fatherhood, the coldness of his message sent chills down my spine. I had Georgia sitting next to me, so I somehow managed to suppress the urge to break down and cry in front of her. Yet here I was alone in the heart of Melbourne, on the other side of the world, discovering I was pregnant and about to become a single mother for the second time. It felt as if Gloria's history was replaying itself in exactly the same city, though I felt my true internal discovery had been in Mark's childhood home in Sydney the day before. Now here I was, carrying the child I had longed for, who was going to be half Australian. I had a torrent of feelings and emotions cascading over me, the strongest of which was unconditional love for the tiny life growing inside me. Terminating the pregnancy was absolutely not an option.

My thoughts were interrupted by a second text from Trickey; this one read "GET RID OF THE VICTIM, YOU'RE 40, YOUR LIFE IS OVER IF YOU HAVE THAT CHILD". This just further intensified the emotional turmoil. His words carried an unseen coldness that shook me to my core. He made it completely clear that he saw this child as a burden rather than a blessing. This stark reality clashed with my profound connection to the life growing inside me. I knew a difficult path lay ahead. I also knew my life wasn't over, instead a new chapter was just beginning.

Our son Cameron Mark was born on 31st October 2011, his middle name Mark obviously given to him as a tribute to his late uncle. I heard via colleagues in the funeral profession that Trickey returned to Australia two weeks before Cameron was born, and we have never seen him since. I know Cameron has a network of grandparents, aunties, uncles and cousins in Australia, but I don't even know if they are aware of his existence. He should also be entitled to dual nationality as his birthright, but alas the lack of presence from his biological father in his life and the fact that I was not even able to include his name on Cameron's birth certificate, means it is highly unlikely that he will ever be able to obtain this.

Both Mum and Dad were absolutely thrilled to become grandparents again. They idolised both of their grandchildren but I know that after going on to have two daughters and a granddaughter, Gloria was overjoyed to have a little baby boy to finally cradle in her arms again.

I of course immediately wrote and told Iris of Cameron's arrival too and let her know that I had chosen his middle name as 'Mark', the name that she too chose to re-name her son at the time of his adoption.

When he was the tender of eight weeks old we celebrated Cameron's naming ceremony and baptism ceremony, an intimate and meaningful occasion shared with our nearest and dearest. We ensured that as his middle name was bestowed on him, in this poignant moment his Uncle Mark was remembered, with the hope and faith that he would forever be watching over and guiding Cameron throughout all of his life. I felt it important to start his life with instilling a sense of connection to his roots, and to the loved ones who might not be physically present in his life, but still held a special place in his journey.

Just one day after Cameron's naming ceremony a package arrived adorned with postage stamps from Australia, and the sender details on the reverse showed it was from Iris. I received it at the front door from the postman and brought it into the living room where Gloria was then sitting next to me on the sofa. I firstly removed the outer layer of brown wrapping paper, then slowly opened the inner layer of white tissue paper. As I did so I glimpsed small reflections of white lace and silk inside. I knew instantly what it was; a lump raced to my throat and tears burned in my eyes. I very carefully took out the contents, lifted it up and showed it to Mum. "Do you recognise this?" I asked her. Of course she recognised it immediately, and burst into tears. I passed it to her to hold, and she held it close to her and whispered, "It's the christening gown I sent with Michael when he was adopted." I hugged her whilst she wept. She had already known her baby had been dressed in this gown on his christening day. Now, once again, just as on the day that Mark had held this gown in his hands for the first time in San Francisco, Gloria felt elation and devastation.

A beautiful letter came with the parcel, but it was the last we ever heard from Iris. We don't know whether she died or whether she felt that returning the christening gown to us was her final act of closure. I subsequently tried to email one of Mark's brothers in Australia but also received no response. I would have liked to have retained contact with them, but also respect their decision to close the door and keep Mark to themselves and within the boundaries of their own family unit.

I was heartbroken that the little christening gown arrived one day too late for Cameron to wear on his naming day. However, six days later on Christmas Day we dressed Cameron in Mark's very special christening gown, and Fr John McCormack, who had conducted his naming ceremony just a week earlier, came to the house and blessed Cameron, the gown and Mark's legacy beneath the twinkling lights of the Christmas tree. Cameron was cocooned in love and the presence of family and friends, so very different to baby Michael/Mark's first Christmas, all alone in the founding home at Waitara.

Six years later, I heard on the grapevine that Trickey went on to father another baby and now embraces the role of a doting dad. His second child was also a little boy and they named him Stanley.

Cameron wearing Mark's christening gown. Christmas Day 2011.

Cameron knows about his little brother, but I don't know whether Stanley knows, or will ever be told about Cameron. It is however another chapter in the replaying of history, in the fact that Cameron now has a half-brother on the other side of the globe with a six-year age gap – exactly the same age gap as there was between me and Mark. It hurts that history is repeating itself in such a way, and I can only hope and pray that one day if the two brothers want to find one another and have a relationship, they will be able to do so.

I have now taken Cameron to Australia on three occasions. He's never met Trickey, nor any of his Australian family as I don't even know of their whereabouts. However, he has been to both Sydney and to Melbourne, he's even visited Featherdale Zoo and fed the kangaroos there in exactly the same way I did on the day I discovered I was pregnant with him. He's walked in the footsteps of his nana, his Uncle Mark, his dad and his little brother. I have made sure he knows and understands his story, his roots and his Australian heritage. He is still young though and whilst he takes it all in his stride, he knows he will always have my 100% support if he ever wants to try to find his Australian family.

Giving birth to Cameron just four days short of my forty-first birthday certainly did not mean my life was over, as Trickey had predicted! On the contrary, it opened up a whole new world of experiences for us. We've travelled extensively, exploring different corners of the globe together. Cameron's education follows a world-schooling approach, akin to home schooling but with an immersive global perspective. This is a journey which has taken us to both North and South America, Europe, Asia, Africa, Australasia, and yes, even Antarctica *(you can read more about our personal travel experiences on www.mumstravelblog. com)* He's grown up happy, healthy, highly sociable, and possesses a genuine love for life, people … and transport!. The penchant for travel seems to be a family trait, as Georgia now works as cabin crew for Virgin Atlantic and gets paid to travel the world. While our journey as a family has had its challenges, I am incredibly proud of the life we've built together, and as a mother, I couldn't be more proud of the remarkable individuals my children have become.

Cameron's upbringing has not lacked a fatherly presence though. Even though I had been separated from Chris for many years when I shared the news of my pregnancy, his immediate response was, "well I've always been here for Georgia and I'll be here for this little one too." True to his word, he attended every antenatal appointment and scan with me, and he was present at Cameron's birth, as was Georgia. Then, with continued and unwavering support, he immediately took on the role of an adoptive daddy to Cameron, in addition to Georgia. Our family unit and co-parenting with my already ex-husband has been very non-conforming but it works, and is a testament to the idea that unconventional can indeed work seamlessly.

I am also delighted to say that after years of experiencing failed and disappointing relationships, my love life does have a very happy ending too (or rather a happy new beginning). In April 2020, amid the challenges of the Covid-19 pandemic, Simon entered my life, having met me online. Georgia by this time already had a house of her own. Exactly one year after meeting Simon, Cameron and I relocated from Sussex to Berkshire to start a new chapter with him and his own three children. Just two months after beginning life together in our new home, Simon asked me to be his wife – of course I answered with a resounding, "yes."

Remarkably, while neither of my children knows their biological fathers, they've found the most incredible love and support in the form of an adoptive father in Chris and a step-father in Simon, both of whom they cherish dearly, and are loved in return. These heart-warming connections emphasise that the power of love can transcend biological ties, creating a rich and supportive family tapestry.

My only regret of course is that societal attitudes toward unmarried mothers in the 1960s were not as supportive as they are today. Gloria's story would have unfolded very differently, and there's a strong possibility that her son might still be alive today. It's a poignant reminder of how other people's perceptions can impact individuals' lives and outcomes.

CHAPTER 14

Sunset and Sunrises

Having been gifted part of Mark's cremated ashes by Clint back in 2010, I kept them close to me at home for several years. I did offer Gloria the chance to take them back to her own home in Wales with her but she insisted they should stay with me, acknowledging the extensive searching and travelling I had done in the quest for my brother. In return however, I did buy her the most beautiful 'mother and child' cremation necklace containing a small portion of those ashes. This way she could carry him around her neck, close to her heart, wherever she went, and she rarely took it off.

Over the years, I have experienced numerous spiritual encounters with Mark. I strongly felt his presence, and very much believed he was a part of guiding me towards meeting his friends and family in various corners of the world, as well as in my everyday life.

One day in 2016 I experienced an especially strong sense of Mark's presence, and felt as if he was asking me to set him free. By now I had held on to his ashes for over six years, yet I instinctively knew it was now time to find him a final resting place. I had made Clint one promise when he gifted me Mark's ashes, that was that I would never bury them. Mark was too much of a free spirit to be kept in a box for eternity. I therefore promised that when the time came to let him go, I would scatter his ashes in an appropriate place, allowing him the freedom to travel, wherever the wind might carry him.

There is a very special place just north of Worthing where I used to live, known as Sleepy Hollow. It's a beautiful woodland glade, with open grassland which is surrounded by tall, strong trees and forests. It is a place which held a special significance in our childhood, a local beauty spot where I know Gloria spent a lot of time when she was young, and where she and Bill would take us when we were growing up. We would have picnics, build forts, walk in the woods and play amidst the bluebells. It held the most simplistic, yet happiest memories. As an adult I have continued this tradition by taking my own children there to do exactly the same. Sleepy Hollow has long been my happy place, my source of solace and my sanctuary. I was sure that if Mark had been raised within our family, this was a place he too would have come to cherish. My heart told me this was a place he would want to be scattered, it would become a sacred spot which we would return to on many occasions with joyful hearts, to walk the dogs, to continue having picnics close to him, and continue creating new and happy memories. It is the location where I, too, want to spend my eternity.

In August 2016 the decision was made, and on a beautiful summer's evening, we gathered at Sleepy Hollow to scatter Mark's ashes. We chose a particular tree, close to the entrance of the forest, where we would often lay down a rug for our picnics. The tree stands where two paths split, ensuring we could easily identify the correct tree in the future. As the sun set, Georgia and Cameron made a mandala around the tree with flowers they had picked from our garden. Then, into the wind, and the hands of the star maker we let Mark go. We knew that although physically he was apart from us, spiritually, he was a part of us.

We return to Sleepy Hollow frequently, sometimes just to stand in silence, sometimes to lay flowers, sometimes to share fun times and picnics, but each time knowing Mark is close by at his final resting place.

For Gloria and Bill, quieter autumn years were now here and both of them spent varying times in and out of hospitals, either with illness, or injuries following falls. Despite the trials, their devotion to each other never wavered. They seamlessly seemed to swap caregiver roles, providing support as one or the other needed help. Bill had always been the healthier and physically stronger one of the pair, but at the end of 2017 his health and strength began to decline rapidly. He'd spent time in hospital at the start of 2018, and two weeks before their golden wedding anniversary we really didn't think he would still be here to mark the occasion. However Dad being Dad, and true to his ever resilient nature, he rallied. Thankfully we managed to get him out of hospital, and home to Gloria, just in time. On March 30th, we celebrated their remarkable fifty years of marriage with a 'quieter than planned' but nevertheless very special golden wedding celebration.

While Dad was never officially diagnosed with dementia, I personally believe he was dealing with Lewys Body Dementia. All the symptoms and signs were there; he faced an ever-continuous decline in both physical ability and mental capacity, although thankfully he always remembered who we were. With Mum and Dad living 230 miles away from us in their retirement years, they were not easily accessible, and I typically only saw them every three to four months. In those latter years, every time I drove from Sussex to Wales I would be filled with the hope of seeing Dad a little fitter and stronger. I desperately longed for the 'old' Dad to resurface, but alas every time I walked through their front door it was the opposite. It was rather like peeling layer after layer off an onion, and in the end only a small core remained of what had once been.

I admit that I struggled terribly watching Dad's demise, and subconsciously I knew it was a contributory factor in my decision to take Cameron off travelling for several months at a time. I just hated witnessing Dad become a shadow of his former self, and I knew he hated it too. Never once did he complain though, as frustrating as he found it. Even though he was now completely housebound and dependent on carers, he would often say to me, "I'm still determined to enjoy my life as best I can. It's better than the alternative." When I wasn't travelling overseas, I spent as much time as possible with Mum and Dad in Wales. To ease their daily lives and lift their spirits, I had a brand new kitchen fitted for them, and bought a motor home so that I could take them out for days without having to worry about stopping for lunches, toilets etc. and risk Dad falling again. These efforts were aimed at providing some comfort and enjoyment amid the challenges they were facing.

Gloria, with her nursing background, embodied the principle of "once a nurse, always a nurse." Despite the fact that they had carers going in to Bill several times a day, she still went above and beyond to provide additional care for her beloved husband. Her dedication and devotion to his well-being enabled him to continue living at home for as long as possible, with her providing the love and reassurance that only a devoted wife could bring.

In August 2019 Bill had been in hospital following yet another fall and was brought home a few days later via hospital transport. Gloria settled him in, made him a cup of coffee and then assisted him through to the bathroom to help him shower as he had come home in the most undignified and filthy condition. Within less than forty-five minutes of being back in the house, tragedy struck as Bill fell backwards in the shower, crashing through the glass screens of the wet room onto the hard floor. Gloria immediately called an ambulance but it took hours to arrive. Unable to lift Bill, she did her best to keep him warm on the wet bathroom floor, wrapping him in towels and duvets until the ambulance finally arrived. This was the breaking point for Gloria, as she knew that she was no longer able to keep Bill safe at home, no matter how hard she tried. The ambulance immediately took him back to hospital, but this time he was sadly never to return home again.

Living in the remote Welsh countryside presented a challenge when it came to finding a suitable nursing home for Bill, especially since Gloria didn't drive, making regular visits almost impossible. After much soul-searching and heartache, the couple made a united decision – they would both move into a nursing home in Somerset, closer to where my sister lived and an area they both loved. Aware that Bill's time on earth was probably fairly limited, Gloria said her intention was to stay with him in the nursing home until his last days, after which she wanted to return to their little home in Wales.

The process, however, was not without its hurdles, as it took months for Social Services to identify a suitable nursing home in a different county and complete all the necessary paperwork. Meanwhile, Bill was sitting in hospital, waiting and waiting, for over four months.

With Bill in hospital, Gloria endeavoured to remain as independent as possible. She missed him dearly, but in all honesty I think in many ways she was also glad of the respite. Bill's care demands often kept her up both day and night, and now at the age of eighty-one herself, she was both physically and mentally exhausted. In the December of the same year, Gloria was heading into town to do some shopping when she had a serious fall stepping off the bus. She too was whisked away to hospital, but unfortunately it was forty miles away from the hospital Bill was in. That morning, as Gloria left the house and caught the bus into town, little did she know that she too would never return to the home they had shared and loved so dearly.

From their respective hospitals in Wales, both Bill and Gloria were finally moved to a nursing home in Somerset just three days before Christmas. Bill settled well and was accepting of his lot. Gloria though was still of very sound mind and reasonable mobility, and she hated it with a passion. She would phone me sobbing and leaving me voicemail messages telling me how desperately unhappy she was. I was desperate to have them living at home with me in Sussex and had even applied for planning permission to build an extension on the side of my house, but the decision to move them into the nursing home had been overruled by my older sister, another tale unto itself.

On 29th February 2020 Gloria unexpectedly suffered a major stroke which left her unable to walk. She was once again hospitalised, leaving Bill alone and increasingly confused in the nursing home. I had just embarked on a three-month trip overseas trip with my son Cameron, and news of Gloria's stroke reached me the day after we had boarded a cruise ship in New Zealand bound for San Diego, USA. This was to be a thirty-five-night voyage across the Pacific Ocean, with stops at some of the most remote islands on the way. Thankfully I was told that Gloria's condition was not life-threatening, but for obvious reasons I couldn't help but worry. Despite the overwhelming feeling of helplessness, I took comfort in the knowledge that both Mum and Dad were in safe hands, receiving the round-the-clock care they each needed, in the appropriate settings.

That same week also marked the end of what any of us considered 'normality' as within days the Covid-19 pandemic began its global shutdown. Cameron and I got stranded on our cruise in the middle of the South Pacific as every port closed its doors, denying entry to our ship, not even allowing us to dock to take on food and fuel. Finally, after a very stressful four weeks at sea and a 'cruise to nowhere', we reached the west coast of America, where weary passengers were finally allowed to back on dry land. We flew straight home to London from San Diego as soon as we were able to disembark the ship, and returned to a new world of lockdown, and the accompanying isolation.

I was desperate to visit my parents, however we faced the harsh reality that their new residence, Wessex House nursing home, along with thousands of other care homes throughout the country, had closed their doors to visitors, enforcing a strict twelve-week lockdown for all residents. Fortunately, Gloria was discharged after a month in hospital, and returned to the nursing home just a couple of days before their lockdown began, so at least she and Bill could be together once again.

Life, however, was not about to give them their lucky break, and just a couple of weeks later it was Bill's turn to be readmitted to hospital. I then received a call at the end of April to be told by nursing staff that Bill was now entering the end-of-life stage, with possibly no more than twenty-four hours left. I immediately got in the car and raced down to Yeovil Hospital which was around a three-hour drive from home. Despite the ongoing lockdown, the hospital fortunately told me they would let me see him, I cannot describe my relief and gratitude, as by now I had not seen him for four months.

Yet there was a major dilemma with Gloria – she was locked down in the care home, but I knew that she had to say goodbye to her husband, I was absolutely not going to let Covid rob her of this. I phoned the manager of the care home and explained what the hospital had just told me, and how we had to let Gloria come to the hospital with me to say her goodbyes. She replied to me by saying, "I'm so sorry, Terri, I'm just not allowed to let Gloria leave this home at the moment, this is the government's ruling, not mine." My heart didn't just sink, it hit the floor. I was absolutely devastated for Mum. However, just as I went through that moment of sheer panic, the manager continued, "what I can do though, is to take her out the front for a little walk, turn my back for a couple of minutes, and you can drive past and kidnap her." I thought she was joking, but she wasn't. Quickly we hatched this plan for me to essentially kidnap my own mother from the doorstep of a nursing home, under cover of darkness. It sounded like a comedy scene from a movie, but it wasn't. Gloria's husband was about to die, and this was the only way she was going to be able to say goodbye to him.

So, at the arranged time, Gloria was 'left' outside the care home in the dark and it was time for me to execute my move. The reality of what I was doing soon became apparent. When I had last seen my mum four months earlier she was fully able bodied, but now she was paralysed from the waist down, and she wasn't a lightweight woman. I hauled her from her wheelchair, almost dropping her on several occasions, and finally managed to manoeuvre her into my car. I folded up the wheelchair, threw it into the boot of the car, and sped away out of sight, as if I had just robbed a bank. Thankfully, despite our deep sadness, we did manage to laugh at the humour and absurdity of it all.

We arrived at the hospital around 10 p.m. and once again I had to try to single-handedly haul Gloria from the car into her wheelchair, and finally within just a few minutes we were both at Bill's bedside holding his hands. We only had an hour or so with him as it was so late in the evening, but given the lockdown, we were grateful to have this. We talked to him, played him music and sang to him. I also swabbed his dehydrated mouth, but all too soon it was time to leave him again. Dad by now had pretty much lost the ability to speak, and hadn't uttered a word the whole time we were there, but as I kissed him goodbye that evening he squeezed my hand with a strength he hadn't had for a very long time, looked me directly in the eye and said in a strong voice, "I've had a lovely life." He knew he was dying and showed no fear, only acceptance.

We didn't want to leave Dad that night but we had to. I drove Gloria back to the nursing home and dropped her in her wheelchair at exactly the same spot where I had 'kidnapped' her from a couple of hours earlier. I phoned the manager and told her we were back, then I hid round the corner and watched until I knew Gloria was safely back inside. I have no idea how many other staff members might have been aware of what happened that night, but I have no words to express my gratitude.

It was by now gone midnight and I was three hours from home, in the middle of lockdown. I couldn't find any accommodation to stay in, as all the hotels and guest houses in the area had been forced to close due to lockdown, so I slept in my car in a lay-by and returned to the hospital the following morning at the crack of dawn.

I was greeted by the ward sister who told me they were sending Bill back to Wessex House as there was no further treatment they could give him there. My sister had also arrived at the hospital by this time, and we knew that was what Dad would want, to be with his beloved Gloria to the end. We of course knew this was what she wanted too. Before he could return there though, they had to have two clear Covid tests from him.

Bill's Covid tests didn't come back in time, and we were told that they wouldn't be able to move him until the following day. Whilst I was grateful for this extra time by his side, I was also scared that he wouldn't make it back to be by Gloria's side again before he passed. Bill was a fighter though and he held on. I spent all that day holding his hand, and gently dropping water and melted ice pops into his mouth, which he seemed to take much relief from.

The hospital had not only ceased treatment but also discontinued all fluids. This little bit of liquid I was now getting into him seemed to be revitalising him, even if it was just in the smallest way. By the evening, I was even able to feed him a little ice cream. I cherish those thirty-six hours I got to be with him so much. Sadly, I had to leave him again that night, and despite returning to the hospital again early the next morning, I found it was time to kiss him goodbye as he made his final ride in the ambulance – back to Wessex House, back to his beloved Gloria.

It meant, however, that I could no longer sit by his side or keep his mouth moist as I had been doing for the past day and a half now. Once he got back to Wessex House, neither Marie nor I would be let inside the doors. It was agonising, but not a decision that the home took lightly. It was the early stage of the pandemic, and the true nature of the virus was still unknown. The residents suffering isolation in care homes had become both a national and international issue, and staff with the best intentions were unable to bend any further rules despite the heartache. The manager continued to do everything she could within the constraints. She moved Bill down from a first-floor room to a ground-floor garden room. This meant that at least we could sit outside his bedroom door, in the garden, and talk to him and sing to him through a partially open window.

Despite that initial prognosis that he might not make the next twenty-four hours, Bill miraculously rallied for another fourteen days, and each day Gloria was brought down to his room to sit with him and hold his hand.

They had one final wish, and it was a poignant one. On the previous Christmas Day, Bill had asked Gloria to renew their wedding vows, and with time now rapidly slipping away, I knew this had to be fulfilled. Being a celebrant myself, I hastily set about crafting a ceremony for them in record time, and Marie went out shopping and bought Bill a new shirt. The care home allowed us to open the patio door for a while, and with Gloria 'the bride' in a mask and full PPE. I renewed their vows through the open door. Bill was too weak to answer with a traditional "I do," but after fifty-two years of marriage, we knew the answer was actually, "I did". He had given his all, he had honoured his marriage vows to the end, and been a devoted husband, father and grandpa; it was an emotional yet beautiful last gift of love to them both, and a moment which we were also able to live-stream to friends and family members around the globe.

The following night, after two weeks of essentially having to watch our father die though a window, we were given the sombre but not unexpected news, that death was now imminent. Whilst sad, it meant that Marie and I were at last allowed into his room to be by his side. Finally, I could hold his hand again. I didn't want to leave that evening and the home told me I could stay, so I spent the whole night lying on the care home floor next to his bed. I didn't get a wink of sleep, but that didn't matter, I had a hold of his hand, and I wasn't letting go. The following day Marie and I rotated our hours with him, as did Gloria, who was visibly exhausted but refused to leave his side. Bill soldiered on as he continued to fight tirelessly to the end. By the next evening I said to Gloria and Marie, "I think he wants to die alone." He had vocalised this in the past, and as we kept our bedside vigil, I could almost hear him shouting in my head, "will you all just piss off and leave me to die in peace," which was very typically Dad!

We all agreed to honour his wish and leave him alone overnight. If he was still alive in the morning, then we would resume our round-the-clock vigil. I bid my goodbyes to him first, as I hadn't slept in more than thirty-six hours. Marie stayed a couple more hours and Gloria sat with him until 23.40hrs when carers came in to take her back up to her room. Just ten minutes later, the carers returned to Gloria to tell her that her darling Bill was dead. He had waited to be alone, and true to his stubborn nature, he did it his own way!

Marie and I immediately returned to Wessex House, where we sat with Dad and comforted Mum until the time came for the funeral directors to come and take him into their care.

The next day, Wessex House granted Marie and me just half an hour to be with Gloria, to discuss and make decisions for Bill's funeral arrangements. We had to meet in the same room where Dad had died the night before, where we now sat staring at an empty bed and stripped mattress. We were all exhausted, heartbroken, and dazed.

After just thirty minutes, the carers came in to take Gloria back to her room, and informed her, "You will not be allowed to see your daughters again now until the funeral." Moreover, as she'd had close contact with us, she had to go into solitary isolation. Consequently, after fifty-two years of marriage, Gloria found herself locked in her room for the next two weeks to grieve for her husband all alone. Marie and I returned to our respective homes to pretty much do the same. I was fortunate in the fact I had my two children to draw some additional strength from.

It was in fact three weeks before the funeral took place and before we could finally see Mum again. In the meantime, I brought Dad's body back to Sussex and into the care of a local funeral home. There, I personally cut his hair, dressed him myself and prepared him for his funeral. I even assisted in lifting him into his coffin.

Then the day came for Bill's funeral. Bill was born into a very impoverished family in Dundee, but as he came into this world as a pauper, I ensured he went out like a king. Even though we were only allowed ten people at his funeral, we held the ceremony in the gardens of a charming little hotel near Yeovil, and he made his final journey in a horse-drawn hearse led by two black stallions. The grand procession was led through the streets by a Scottish bagpiper. Marie then helped to carry his coffin from the hearse to the gardens, and I conducted his Celebration of Life ceremony. He would have loved it all.

Despite our sorrow, we celebrated Bill's life with the most joyous memories, which is exactly how we knew he would want it to be. Gloria had been instructed by Wessex House that she was not allowed to hug her family when she came out to the funeral, but how could we not hug our own mother on the day of our father's funeral? Especially knowing the grief and isolation she had been through since the day of his death. She needed hugs and so did we, so I'm not ashamed to say she had plenty of hugs that day. However, given her contact with the outside world, we all knew what awaited her when she returned to the care home…another two weeks of bedroom isolation. It was agony. I wanted to whisk her up and take her back to her home to Wales which is what she desperately wanted too, but her recent stroke had robbed her of her mobility, making it impossible. Having initially said that she had only been going to move into a care home with Bill until he passed, but she was the one who now needed the round-the-clock care.

More heartache was to follow. Bill and Gloria had been able to take their little cat Felix to live in Wessex House with them, but forty-eight after Bill's funeral the new manager told her she was no longer allowed to keep her cat. Felix was all she had left there, her sole companion and source of comfort. In less than six months Gloria had lost her home, her mobility, her freedom and her husband, now she was being forced to give up the one thing she had left there, Felix. Her heart was broken and ours broke for her. It was so cruel and unfair, and yet we were completely helpless. Felix went to live with Marie, in the hope that Gloria would later be able to visit him there. We needed to grieve as a family, but we couldn't. By now we were seven weeks into the initial twelve-week lockdown for care homes. "Just five more weeks, Mum," I said to her on the phone, "be brave and be strong, we need you as much as you need us, very soon we'll all be back together."

Five weeks came and went, yet care homes remained locked down. Wessex House did arrange for Gloria to have a daily video call with us, and Marie and I alternated this every morning at 10 a.m. to lift her spirits up a little. However, emotionally she was struggling. The reality of losing Bill, along with the prospect that she would now be confined to a wheelchair and stuck in a nursing home for the rest of her life, was devastating for her.

Without the lockdown, we could have made that time so much better for her. She had two daughters who loved her, and would have taken her out for drives, walks in her wheelchair, shopping trips and picnics by the local river. I even started the process of buying a second home in Somerset to be closer to her. We were to be just a mile from her geographically when we stayed there yet were banned from being able to see her.

As the weeks and months ticked on, we were granted just a little more freedom. Gloria was allowed a thirty-minute garden visit once a week, something which once again Marie and I would alternate. I would drive a 250-mile round trip between Sussex and Somerset just for that treasured half an hour, once a fortnight. We both cherished every second because never before had time been so precious, yet the minutes went so quickly and Mum understandably hated it when I had to leave. I would drive home every time with tears streaming down my face.

On a few occasions, Gloria had outpatient appointments to attend at the hospital, but each time she left Wessex House she then faced a mandatory two-week bedroom isolation, and her visits from us were prohibited during that time. We worked out that from Bill's death on 15th May to her next in-patient stay in hospital at the end of October, Gloria had spent a total of eleven weeks in complete isolation at Wessex House. Locked up like a prisoner for doing no wrong. She had been forced to grieve her son's adoption in silence, forced to grieve his death in private and now she was being forced to grieve her husband's death in isolation. It felt so cruel and so very wrong.

On 29th October 2020, Gloria was admitted to Yeovil hospital for a small procedure on her bladder which we knew would necessitate an overnight stay post-surgery. Although the operation itself was fairly uncomplicated, the primary concern lay in the anaesthetic, particularly given Gloria's age of eighty-two, and her previous medical history. She had been enduring significant pain though and grappling with multiple bladder infections. As a former nurse with her extensive experience, she knew all the risks, and the decision to go ahead with the surgery was 100% her own. We therefore breathed a huge sigh of relief later that day when were told that she had come round from the anaesthetic and was doing well. Marie was allowed a brief visit to see her, and told me that she was lucid, happy and chatty, and looking forward to returning to Wessex House the next day.

However, the next morning brought an unexpected development when we received a call from the hospital, informing us that Gloria was being transferred to a 'hot ward.' She had developed a fever and was experiencing some respiratory difficulties. This particular ward was designated for patients suspected of having Covid-19. Despite Gloria having tested negative for Covid-19 both the day before and on the day of her admission, she was moved to this isolation ward as a precautionary measure. Unfortunately, the strict protocols in place meant that visitors were not permitted under any circumstances.

Naturally, we were not only concerned about Gloria's condition, but now had the additional fear of her contracting Covid-19. We fought with considerable effort to get her out of that ward, and after around five days she continued to test negative for Covid-19. On my fiftieth birthday she was transferred back to a regular ward which meant that I would be able to visit her. It was the best birthday present I could have asked for, and it goes without saying that Gloria was over the moon. Even though that visit was limited to just fifteen minutes, she was beyond excited that she had been able to share a part of my big day with me, especially since I had made the three-hour drive to be by her side – and, best of all, to bring her some birthday cake! Unfortunately, we already knew that day that with the resurgence of Covid-19 cases, hospitals nationwide were having to reinstate full lockdown measures the next day, depriving Gloria and so many other patient of any further visits for the foreseeable future. It broke both of our hearts, when after spending just fifteen minutes together on my birthday, we kissed goodbye, not knowing how long it was going to be until we would be allowed to see one other again.

A few days later, Gloria was scheduled to return Wessex House as thankfully her health was improving. I was due to go down and pick her up, and she telephoned me that morning saying she hadn't slept all night as she was so excited to see me and to be returning to Wessex House, as she had come to really love some of the staff there. However, whilst I was on the long drive back to collect her, I received another distressing telephone call from the manager at Wessex House informing me that both they and Gloria's hospital ward were now experiencing an outbreak of Covid-19, and no one was being moved either in or out. Gloria was going nowhere, her planned discharge abruptly halted.

When I called to inform her, she was beyond distraught, and I could tell that she was now beginning to give up on life. Just an hour or so later, she called me back again and was sobbing down the phone, saying, "I can't go on, I just can't, I don't want to be here anymore if this is going to be my life. You need to just get on with your lives and your future happiness now." In my own heartbreak I pleaded with her once again, "please, Mum, don't give up now, it's all going to be OK really soon. Happier days are coming," I told her, but they weren't.

A week later Gloria received the diagnosis of Covid-19, and a couple of days after that she suffered a major haemorrhage. To this day, it remains unclear to us whether Covid-19 was a contributing factor to this or not. However, without any discussion with Marie or me, the medical team made the decision to withdraw Gloria's anti-stroke medication. Marie and I (being denied any hospital visits) were completely unaware of this until eight days later when we received a call from the hospital informing us that Gloria had suffered another stroke and had been found unresponsive in her hospital bed. Marie rushed to the hospital promptly, whilst I embarked on yet another three-hour mercy drive from Sussex to be by her side as soon as soon as I could.

I have to say that the nursing staff on this ward were beyond phenomenal, and they could not have done any more, either for Gloria or us, especially given that the hospital was still on full lockdown. Gloria regained consciousness, although she had pretty much lost the ability to speak and to swallow, but she knew we were there by her side. The nurses on duty bent the lockdown rules enabling us to go in three times a day for an hour as her carers. Gloria was now being fed puréed food, but it took ages for her to even attempt to eat each meal. The nursing staff naturally couldn't dedicate the time to do this, so Marie and I spent hours with her each day lovingly feeding her every morsel of food. She tried so hard to get it down, despite pulling faces and mouthing "yuk" after every mouthful.

After a week of us rotating our feeding shifts at Gloria's bedside, one of the doctors came in and said they needed to speak to Marie and me together. We immediately sensed the gravity of the situation, but we couldn't bring ourselves to hear it. It had been less than seven months since Dad had died, and our grief was still so raw as we had had no opportunity to process it properly. We were doing all we could simply to just get through our first Christmas without him. Sitting there numb in the doctor's office, we braced ourselves for the inevitable, as the doctor and ward sister addressed us. "Your mum isn't getting any better, she isn't responding to treatment, we need to withdraw treatment and let her go." The news was unbearable, the physical pain as well as the emotional agony excruciating. As much as I hurt when Dad died, I had been prepared for it as he'd been ill for so long, but with Mum I wasn't ready. We still hadn't had our time together as a family to grieve for Dad. Gloria had been imprisoned and isolated between a care home and a hospital for the last seven months. I found myself repeating over and over again, "this isn't fair, it isn't fair." This horrific time could not mark the end of her life, it just couldn't.

Mum's Christmas presents were wrapped neatly wrapped under the Christmas tree. Marie and I had taken care of her Christmas shopping, selecting gifts from her, for each other, and for her to give the grandchildren. There was no way we could now watch her die and then go home to these unopened presents. Thus, Christmas came early for us. We dashed home, got some decorations and lights to adorn her now private side room in the hospital, and came back with her presents, which we then opened at her bedside. Though she was barely conscious at this point, we like to think she was aware somewhere deep within, and conscious of the moment.

Marie slept on a camp bed in her hospital room, and I stayed locally until the next morning. Together, we dedicated the entire following day to be with her. She was washed with her new Christmas soap, and adorned with her new co-ordinating perfume, and the very last thing to touch her lips was a drop of Baileys Irish Cream – something she would most definitely have approved of. Georgia drove down from Sussex to say her final goodbyes to her Nana with my then 'partner' Simon joining us, holding her hand and promising Gloria he would take care of me forever.

The hospital chaplain was restricted from conducting ward visits due to Covid-19. Nevertheless, I received the words of the Last Rites from another friend of mine who is a vicar. I knew this would be an important rite for Gloria as she transitioned, as although she had stopped going to church some years earlier, her faith remained important to her. I sat and read the Last Rites and some appropriate prayers to her, as I gently stroked her cheek. I assured her that it was alright to let go, that Marie and I would be OK, as would Georgia and Cameron. I told her that Bill, Michael (Mark) and her mum and dad were already waiting for her, and would all be ready for a joyous reunion. I comforted her with the thought that she would finally be able to hold her beautiful baby boy in her arms, and cradle him once again.

At 5.40pm on 16th December 2020, with Marie and me by her side, and with the ironic backdrop of Vivaldi's 'Gloria' playing, Gloria drew her final breath beneath the twinkling Christmas lights, and acquired her angelic wings. She went home to reunite with her beloved Bill, and to find the joy in spending her first ever Christmas with her son.

Suddenly, we were orphaned, and completely bereft. In the span of just seven months, amid a global pandemic and the isolating effects it brought, we experienced the profound loss of both our parents.

When your parents reach their eighties, you anticipate a time will come when they will no longer be with you, but losing them both so close together, in the time and manner we did, was beyond comprehension. Despite my then eighteen years working in the funeral profession, I was at a loss as to how to even begin processing and healing from this intense grief. On Christmas Eve, I found myself in the funeral director's chapel of rest, tenderly and lovingly preparing Gloria's cold form, dressing her with care, and ensuring she looked her very best for Christmas Day. Yet it broke my heart to confront the harsh reality that she would actually be spending Christmas Day alone, and in the fridge of the funeral home mortuary.

Just like we had held for Dad, we gave Mum the most incredible send-off despite the ongoing lockdown restrictions. We held her funeral on January 8th, coinciding with what would have been Dad's eighty-sixth birthday, and our first one without him. It also commemorated the fifty-fourth anniversary of Gloria and Bill's first date. Gloria's Celebration of Life ceremony was held in a rustic barn back in Worthing, the town in which she had spent sixty years of her life. Her final journey was not in a traditional hearse, but in an old Australian farm truck, and on her coffin a scene depicted Sydney Harbour Bridge, just as she had asked for a decade previously when she had seen Mark's ashes casket featuring the Golden Gate Bridge.

We had previously been awaiting Mum's release from lockdown before fulfilling her wish to scatter Dad's ashes close to Mark's in Sleepy Hollow. However, this poignant act was still pending, and now with both parents' cremains in our possession, the moment had finally arrived. Choosing the date which would have been their fifty-third wedding anniversary on March 30th, we set out on an early morning drive to Sleepy Hollow, and as the sun ascended, shining its light onto a brand new day, we lovingly scattered their ashes together, alongside Mark's. The three of them were now together for eternity.

Whilst we dispersed all of Bill's ashes, we reserved about 25% of Gloria's. A huge part of her heart had always remained in Australia, and she had always longed to go back there. So deep within, I knew there was just one more journey I had to make. A part of Gloria would return to Australia.

Gloria's funeral, January 2021

CHAPTER 15

I Still Call Australia Home

As at the day of writing this final chapter, 29th November 2022, it will be exactly twenty years since my brother Mark (born Michael William Bayliss) died from AIDS. I dedicate this whole story both to him and to our mother, Gloria Kivlichan (nee Bayliss). I also dedicate this to all those who lost their lives throughout the AIDS and Covid-19 pandemics.

Amidst the heartache, isolation and losses that defined 2020, I also consider myself incredibly fortunate to have met my soul mate Simon. Strangely, it was at a time when I was truly happy being independent and single, yet Cupid clearly had other ideas. Actually, meeting Simon (online) in the early part of lockdown proved to be a silver lining that marked a turning point in my love life. Let's face it, given my own history, I could quite easily imagine penning a whole other book chronicling my experiences of failed relationships and dating disasters.

Simon and I recognised the depth of our connection very early on in our relationship and knew that we wanted to spend the rest of our lives together. We had spoken about the prospect of marriage on numerous occasions before we ever formally got engaged.

I knew following Gloria's death, that I wanted to take some of her ashes back to Australia. I had absolute certainty that this is what she would have wanted too. As we sifted through her personal belongings after her room had been cleared at Wessex House, we found a newspaper cutting advertising a trip to Australia, on which she had written "I can finally go back to Australia once Covid is over". The article was dated after Bill's death. On one of my garden visits during the previous months she had also told me that she had seen a rail trip across Australia advertised and really wanted to do it. Remarkably, this determination to return to the land she loved persisted despite her frailty and wheel-chair-bound state, following her first stroke. It proved to us that she had never given up on her dream of returning there.

With this in mind, I tentatively broached the idea with Simon of marrying in Sydney at the same time we scattered Mum's ashes, and he instantly replied with an enthusiastic "yes" (it wasn't a proposal, merely a question!). Simon got down on one knee and formally proposed to me about six months later – I also replied with an enthusiastic "yes."

The more I thought about it, the more the prospect of a wedding in Sydney grew in its significance. Sydney held a multitude of meaningful connections; it was Mark's birthplace, the departure point for Gloria's 1966 sail home to England, and the destination she always yearned to revisit. It was also where I first learned of my pregnancy with Cameron, and a city that had cradled countless dreams since my childhood.

Additionally, I knew that a portion of Mark's ashes had been taken back to Sydney by Iris after his funeral, and although we never knew his final resting place on that side of the globe, just knowing that he was somewhere close within the suburbs of Sydney added another poignant layer of symbolism. I yearned to now marry the man of my dreams in this cherished city and complete a very long and complex circle of love. I was so grateful too that Simon also shared in my vision and was determined to enable my dream to come true.

Initially, Simon and I discussed the idea of taking all five of our children to Australia for our wedding. However, as we delved into the practical and social intricacies, we realised it would not only be a costly endeavour but also logistically unfeasible. On the very same day Gloria suffered her final stroke, Simon's daughter, at the age of just nineteen, suffered a serious blood clot in her leg at a result of long Covid, and almost lost her leg. Medical advice ruled out long-haul flights due to the risk of deep vein thrombosis. Additionally, Simon's dad would be ninety-five by the time our wedding arrived and would not be able to undertake such a long journey either.

It was important to both Simon and me to have our entire immediate family with us on such a special day, we therefore opted for a dual celebration – a larger scale ceremony at home in the UK with all our friends and family, just without the formal signing of the marriage register. We would then hold a more intimate legal ceremony around Sydney Harbour, coinciding with the scattering of Gloria's ashes in the same vicinity. This arrangement would ensure that our special days embraced both our extensive circle of loved ones, and the poignant ties to Sydney.

As I mentioned in the preceding chapter, Cameron and I ended up on a four-week 'cruise to nowhere' when the Covid-19 pandemic struck in March 2020. Consequently, Holland America Line granted us a future cruise credit of the equivalent value which had to be used by the end of 2022. We had waited and waited for cruising to resume again, then quickly found the perfect voyage, a transpacific journey, retracing the route we took in 2020 but in reverse. Instead of departing from Auckland to San Diego, as we did previously, this new cruise would take us from San Diego to Sydney, departing in October 2022.

It felt as if the stars were aligning. Given that Gloria had sailed out of Sydney in 1966, I could now, in 2022, sail her back into the harbour that she so loved. When she tearfully left those waters in 1966, leaving her baby son behind, she could never have imagined that fifty-six years later, she would one day have a daughter and grandson who would guide her return. As heart-breaking as losing her had been, it felt like the most perfect and loving conclusion to both her and Mark's stories.

Mum loved cruising too, and she and Dad had embarked on numerous cruises during their retirement years, since Dad refused to fly. I knew she would have just loved this final voyage and all the symbolism which was now to be woven into its course.

Since it had only been Cameron and me who had made the transpacific voyage in 2020, naturally we were the only recipients of the cruise credit. Additionally, Simon could not be away from his business and his own children for that extended period. It would mean us being apart for six weeks, but he had known that this was on the horizon since the day we met, and we were more than confident that our love was strong enough to endure both the time and distance. Moreover, as a bonus we had something incredibly special to look forward to when we would finally be reunited in Sydney.

On 2nd September we celebrated our wedding ceremony in the UK. It unfolded as a perfect day, with the ceremony conducted by Samantha Pitt, an exceptional celebrant whom I had personally trained a few years prior, and which added yet another very special layer of magic to the occasion. Simon and I pledged our love and commitment to one another and exchanged wedding rings by the banks of the River Thames, surrounded by the love of around sixty of our family members and closest friends. We then hosted our reception on a passenger boat sailing up the river. To transport me to my wedding I chose the same pair of black horses, Joker and Jester, along with their carriage master Sonny Hillier, which had carried my father on his final journey to his funeral two and a half years earlier. Although Dad was not there to walk me down the aisle, it felt as though this represented part of his onward journey. On my wrist I wore a bangle which contained just a tiny bit of both Mum and Dad's ashes, and around my neck I wore Mum's necklace which contained some of Mark's ashes. Ensuring they were all with us on our special day.

Simon and I enjoyed just three weeks of married life together before Cameron and I were off on our travels. I carefully packed up Gloria's ashes, carrying them in my hand luggage as my most precious cargo. Although I ensured I had all the necessary paperwork with me, I was still convinced that as I carried this white powder through customs someone was going to stop me for attempted drug smuggling! Fortunately, at no stage did we encounter any problems.

We spent a week between Los Angeles and San Diego, and then, two and half years after disembarking from the Maasdam in the same city, it was finally time to board her sister ship Noordam, to complete

our transpacific adventure. Both Cameron and I were filled with excitement as we boarded the ship, although I couldn't help but reflect on the significant events which had unfolded between the two cruises in a relatively short space of time. We had weathered a global pandemic, I had lost both of my parents, and I had met and married the man of my dreams. It felt like a very different world to the one we had left there in 2020. Hurriedly making our way to our cabin, we began to unpack for our five-week voyage, I took out the small cardboard scatter tube containing Gloria's ashes and popped them on the dressing table with a view out over the balcony. A few hours later, the Noordam sounded her horn and we sailed away from the coast of California. Gloria had begun her epic final voyage.

Over the next five weeks we sailed the Pacific waters, visiting the most idyllic destinations, which included Hawaii, French Polynesia, the Cook Islands, Tonga, New Caledonia and Brisbane, before ultimately arriving in Sydney. In the early morning sunrise as we sailed in past the iconic Opera House, and under the majestic Harbour Bridge that held such a special place in Gloria's heart, I retreated quietly to our cabin alone. Holding Gloria's ashes tube in my hands, I whispered to her, "Welcome home, Mum" – I heard her reassuring voice whisper right back in my ear, "No one could have done more."

I hoped she was right, I was yearning to believe I had done her proud.

Simon had flown out to Sydney and stood there on the dockside to greet us. For years, I had envisioned my brother welcoming me to Sydney with open arms, but this time, I found myself embraced by another man. A man who not only understood my story but also Mark's and Gloria's stories, and a man who was now going to be a part of weaving these together to a beautiful conclusion.

Over the next couple of days we visited some significant places around Sydney; we discovered the hospital where Gloria had given birth to Mark, and we drove out to the Blue Mountains, stopping at the village which had been Mark's first childhood home.

Two days after we had sailed into the waters of Sydney, on a warm, sunny but windy day, Simon and I legally married on a catamaran in Sydney Harbour. This second ceremony was officiated by celebrant Roxy Hotten, whom I had also trained several years earlier. Roxy had flown in from Brisbane especially to do the honours, which meant so much to us. It was a much smaller ceremony with just five other guests in attendance, my two cousins, and three friends whom Cameron and I had originally met on our 2020 cruise, and with whom we had just shared another five weeks on our latest voyage. It was the most perfect and intimate setting.

Simon and I reaffirmed the tender vows which we had spoken two months earlier. Simon then presented me with a breath-taking eternity ring, its diamonds reset from my late grandmother's eternity ring, truly the icing on the cake.

As we ended the ceremony, I tearfully scattered Gloria's ashes into the waters of the harbour, directly below where Simon and I had just sealed our lifelong commitment. Her much loved Harbour Bridge stood proud in the background. As we scattered her ashes, we played the song 'I still call Australia Home' by Hugh Jackman, one of the same songs we had also played at her funeral.

In my bouquet nestled three sunflowers: one for Mark, one for Gloria and one for Bill. I plucked them from the bouquet and one by one I lovingly let them fall into the waters, to drift a while with Gloria's ashes to wherever the winds and the tide might carry them.

This final act of devotion was the most loving gesture I could think of giving to my mum, and the most perfect way to honour my brother's life and his existence in this world. It was also the most positive and uplifting finale to a story which had been marked with so much sadness. It was the end of one chapter, but the beginning of a brand new one. One which I know Mum (and Dad) would have wholeheartedly given their blessing to.

Gloria was finally home in Australia, and now at peace. After fifty-eight years the circle of love was now complete.

GLORIA 1938 – 2020

About the Author

Terri Negus is a highly respected civil celebrant and esteemed trainer in the United Kingdom. As the founder and director of the Fellowship of Professional Celebrants, she has made significant contributions to the field. With over two decades of experience crafting and narrating ceremonies that beautifully capture the life stories of others, Terri has now embarked on a deeply personal journey to share a compelling true story of her own.

Inspired by her mothers emigration adventure to Australia and the subsequent events that altered the course of her own life, Terri brings a unique perspective and emotional depth to her writing in her debut book.

Printed in Great Britain
by Amazon

45797805R00066